WARREN BUFFETT'S
Secret Millionaires Club®

HOW TO START
YOUR VERY FIRST
BUSINESS

From the producers of
Warren Buffett's Secret Millionaires Club

with Julie Merberg and Sarah Parvis

downtown 🏙 bookworks

Copyright © 2015 by Downtown Bookworks Inc.

Published by Downtown Bookworks Inc.

Cover and interior designed by Georgia Rucker.

Downtown Bookworks Inc.
265 Canal Street
New York, NY 10013
www.dtbwpub.com

For more great business advice, check out www.smckids.com.

Warren Buffett's Secret Millionaires Club trademark, illustrations,
and logo are the property of Genius Brands International, Inc.
Used with permission.

Cover photo of cell phone: © Shutterstock.com/cobalt88.

Images of Square Reader courtesy of Square.

FOREWORD

Success in business depends on good habits that are formed early in life.

In the Secret Millionaires Club, we have tried to share valuable lessons, which will help you be successful not just in business but in life. Learning the value of being honest, being willing to take risks and fail, and protecting your reputation are among the lessons that form the fabric of success. The importance of these lessons, along with hard work and character, cannot be overstated. Those who learn these lessons early will go on to great accomplishments.

Good luck, Secret Millionaires, and never forget, the best investment you can make is an investment in yourself.

—Warren Buffett

CONTENTS

INTRODUCTION

What Is Business and What Will You Need to Get Started?

The nature of business is to make a product or service that meets the public's needs and to profit (make money) from the sale of this product or service. You don't need tons of money and a fancy suit to start a business. All you need is some imagination and a willingness to work hard and learn.

An entrepreneur is someone who starts and runs his or her own business. That person is usually pretty brave because starting a business can be risky. In the business world, entrepreneurs are often called "risk takers." Warren Buffett is a risk taker, but he doesn't believe in taking foolish risks. The lessons in this book will help you make smart choices and give you a better chance of earning your success.

Inside, you'll find lots of ideas for ways to earn money. You will also get simple, step-by-step advice for starting your very first business—whether you're walking dogs, building websites, or doing something else entirely. And you will learn how to save, spend, and invest the money you earn. You will have the benefit of Warren Buffett's wisdom, along with inspiring stories (true ones!) about kids just like you—who had an idea and turned it into a business.

CHAPTER 1

WHAT CAN I DO?
SELLING STUFF

Your very first business transaction probably involved trading something. Maybe you traded your lunch with another kid at school. Or you traded toys, books, or video games with friends or a brother or sister.

If you've ever been involved in an exchange like this, you've already conducted business. With this book, you are just going to learn how to do it better. The more you learn and the more you practice, the better you'll get.

Businesses generally engage in two types of trade: selling things and selling services. First, let's look at selling stuff, or products.

Warren Buffett's Very First Business

You might be surprised that one of the most successful businessmen in the world started his first business when he was just 6 years old. It was a small business based on a simple idea. Warren would buy things in **bulk** (a lot at a time) and then resell them individually (one at a time). He knew that if he could sell things like packs of chewing gum for more than he had paid for them, he would make a **profit**.

He started by buying six-packs of soda for 25 cents and then reselling each can for a nickel. He went on to sell gum from his grandfather's grocery store door to door. He grew his business—and his business skills—from there. Everybody starts somewhere.

It's Never Too Early to Get Started

Selling things that you own, make, or buy is one of the easiest and most common ways to start making money. In many cities and towns, people have stoop sales or yard sales, where they spread out their gently used toys, books, or clothing and sell them for a fraction of what they cost originally—right in front of their own homes. In cities, depending on the area, there can be a lot of "foot traffic"—people walking by who will easily see the items being sold. In warm weather, it's common to see lemonade stands or bake sales outdoors. These are all great ways to make money. And the Internet has provided even more "places" to sell things.

Lots of kids your age have started businesses selling lemonade, homemade crafts, books, toys, and other items. Some kids have turned these small businesses into big businesses. What business is right for you?

bulk

a large quantity of something, usually bought at a lower price than it would cost to buy the same thing one at a time or in small quantities

profit

the money you make in business once you've subtracted the cost of your supplies or other expenses. For example, Warren Buffett bought six cans of soda for 25 cents and then sold them for a total of 30 cents. By subtracting his cost (25 cents) from what he resold the cans for (30 cents), he had a **profit** of 5 cents for each six-pack.

WORDS FROM WARREN

Can you really explain to a fish what it's like to walk on land? One day on land is worth a thousand years of talking about it, and one day running a business has exactly the same kind of value.

Turn Something You Love Into a Business

Are you artistic or crafty? Can you sew or paint? Do you enjoy making jewelry or personalizing hats? Are you a wonderful cook? Does your family have a great tradition or recipe that you'd like to share with the world? Are there any products you really like that you want to dedicate yourself to selling better and smarter than the stores near you do?

When you are thinking about a possible product to sell, first look to the things you like best. If you love fishing, you could raise worms for bait or sell hand-painted fishing lures. If you are a dancer, you might consider knitting leg warmers, personalizing leotards, or making hair accessories for ballet buns. Are you a computer-savvy sports fan? You could create, print, and sell stickers and decals in the colors of your local teams.

Cameron Johnson enjoyed making invitations and greeting cards for his family to use for celebrations. Pretty soon, friends, family, and his parents' coworkers wanted to buy this 9-year-old's one-of-a-kind cards. Cameron turned a hobby he enjoyed into a money-making business called Cheers and Tears.

Moziah Bridges was a stylish young man who liked to wear bow ties. But he couldn't find any with cool designs that looked right for him. So at the age of 9, he started using his grandmother's scrap fabric to design his own. Soon he began selling his handmade, funky bow ties through the online marketplace Etsy.com. Now Mo's Bows are sold in many stores and on the Neiman Marcus website.

WORDS FROM WARREN

In the world of business, the people who are most successful are those who are doing what they love.

Fill a Need

Lots of kids (and adults too) have started great businesses simply by noticing that their friends, family, and community needed something. They stepped in to fill a need, and a business was born!

markup

the amount of money added to a product's cost to cover both expenses and profit. If you buy a product and then resell it, you will have to charge your customers more for the item than you paid for it in order to make a profit. That additional charge is called a **markup**.

Many people are concerned about the ingredients in their shampoos and conditioners. They want to use natural hair-care products. Lucky for **Leanna Archer**, she had just the product to fill that need. Her Haitian great-grandmother had a secret recipe for all-natural hair pomade that Leanna used and loved. At age 9, she was her own best advertisement without even trying to be. Friends complimented her hair, and she gave them samples of her homemade pomade. Soon, they wanted more. Leanna convinced her parents that she needed to start selling this product online. The business became so successful that Leanna now sells a complete line of beauty and hair-care products—Leanna's All Natural Hair Products—and her father quit his job to help Leanna full-time.

From Baseball Cards to Basketball Teams

Today, Mark Cuban is the billionaire owner of a basketball team (the Dallas Mavericks). He also owns movie theaters, a film company, and other investments. But Mark didn't start out there. He had his first business when he was only about 9 years old. He noticed that all of his friends were collecting baseball cards. Baseball cards were the need, and he could provide them. Mark bought the cards in bulk, repackaged them, added a markup, and sold them to his friends for a profit.

Mark started his next business because he wanted new basketball shoes. A family friend wanted to get rid of some extra garbage bags and gave them to the entrepreneurial 12-year-old. Mark decided to try selling them door to door. It turned out that lots of people needed garbage bags, and Mark was able to buy his sneakers with the income from his door-to-door trash bag business.

Katelyn Lohr's business grew out of her own need. She wanted socks to wear with flip-flops. Toeless socks, that is. At the age of 8, she designed her own and wore them to school, where her friends saw them and wanted some too. Katelyn called her toeless socks Freetoes and began selling them to her classmates and teachers. Then she sold them in local markets. Now they are sold in stores throughout North America.

A New Take on an Old Standby

You do not have to invent a whole new product to have a successful business. Sometimes making a small improvement or adjustment to an already existing product can make an enormous difference.

The summer when **Abi Smithson** was just 8 years old, she noticed weird marks on her mom's feet. They were tan lines from the sandals she'd been wearing. If wearing sandals in the sun is going to give you tan lines, Abi thought, it would be better if the patterns were prettier! She went to work and developed the Love Sandal, which features a heart-shaped cutout in the leather strap. That way, if the wearer gets a tan line, it will be in the sweet shape of a heart.

aha moment

when you suddenly have
a great idea or realization

At 9 years old, **Greyson MacLean** liked to build with Lego bricks. But he didn't like the stickers that came with the Lego sets. Once you stuck them on, you couldn't remove them or reposition them. At first, he made his own images and taped them onto Lego bricks. But then his mother bought a new pair of sunglasses and noticed the decals on her glasses peeled right off. It was just the aha moment they needed!

Now Greyson and his family make reusable stickers and cling decals for Lego and other building toys. They took an already existing product (stickers for building bricks) and made a slight change (now they are removable and reusable!) and turned a simple idea into a successful business. Greyson's BrickStix come in all sorts of themes (space, pets, commandos, zombies, castles, towns, and more) and are sold at BrickStix.com, Amazon.com, and other retailers.

Abi's Love Sandal and Greyson's BrickStix are examples of common items that have been made better with a simple tweak. Think of the products you and your family own. How can you improve them? Is there a modern take or design change that might make you like an item even more than you already do?

13

Find New Customers for a Popular Product

Some great businesses are successful because they offer a new spin that attracts a whole new kind of customer.

Hart Main was just 13 years old when his little sister started selling candles for a fundraiser. Hart didn't really like the vanilla- or lavender-scented candles that she was selling. He joked that more guys would buy candles if they came in different scents. So Hart got to work, coming up with smells like sawdust, bacon, coffee, and baseball mitt. And then he came up with a great name for his product: ManCans. Soon Hart had his own popular online shop, and he couldn't keep up with all the orders.

WORDS FROM WARREN

Always think of alternative ideas and new ways of doing things.

Big Companies, New Customers

Big companies look for new customers for their existing products too. The Lego company noticed that almost all of its toys were purchased by boys. They wanted girls to start buying them too. So they asked girls what they wanted to build. They listened to their responses and developed new Lego toys, using different-colored bricks and female characters. They also created new building projects, like a tree house, a veterinarian's office, a horse show, and a two-story-tall yacht.

At 14 years old, **Jake Johnson** was already a bow tie fan. But not many kids his age wear bow ties. Many kids think of bow ties as something their grandfathers wear. Jake thought kids might be more interested in bow ties if they looked a little different from grandpa's. So he and his sister **Lachlan** came up with an inventive twist on the classic bow tie. They cut the bow tie in half and developed a clip that allows the wearer to attach two different halves together. That way, users can mix and match colors, patterns, and fabrics for a look all their own. This simple yet clever take on the bow tie makes it appeal to a younger consumer—the kind of consumer who values personalization over tradition. Many people—including Warren Buffett—are fans. In fact, Jake was the individual grand prize winner of the 2014 Warren Buffett's Secret Millionaires Club "Grow Your Own Business Challenge." Jake and Lachlan's successful bow-tie business is called Beaux Up.

Can you think of a toy, game, gift, food, or item of clothing that could find a new audience if it was changed in some simple way?

Grab a Pen and Start Brainstorming!

Write down the things you like to make. Write down the things you use when you practice your favorite hobbies and activities. Write down the products you and your friends like. Write down the items you think your community needs. Do you see any business ideas on your list? Can you think of a way to improve on the products available? Keep adding to the list and **brainstorming** until something feels just right.

brainstorming
coming up with creative ideas or solutions to problems by thinking of lots of ideas and suggestions. No idea is too wacky during a **brainstorm**. You can see if your crazy idea is possible or practical later.

What Do You Like to Do?

Here are a bunch of ideas for products that are related to popular hobbies, habits, and sports. Fill in the chart with things you like to do and possible product ideas.

THINGS I LIKE TO DO	RELATED PRODUCTS THAT I COULD MAKE AND SELL
Gardening	I could grow herbs in little containers and sell them to my neighbors. Or I could grow flowers and sell bouquets of fresh flowers.
Building things	I could build and decorate birdhouses or bat houses.
Hockey	I could paint hockey pucks with cool pictures or with the names of teams and the dates of important games.
Rock collecting	I could paint rocks in bright patterns or to look like fairies, monsters, or animals to decorate people's gardens. I could paint letters or numbers on rocks. These rocks could spell out people's last names or house numbers and be used as lawn markers.
Bicycling	I could make license plates for bikes.

A Few of My Favorite Things

Do you collect stickers? Love to wear funky shoelaces?
Fill in the chart below with products you like and ways
you could make them new, different, or better.

ITEMS I LIKE	WAYS TO CHANGE OR IMPROVE THEM
Friendship bracelets	I could make them with out-of-the-ordinary supplies, like metallic or glow-in-the-dark thread. I could add charms to the friendship bracelets or sew on tiny pockets that could hold messages or quotes.
Stuffed animals	I could make jewelry, crowns, and tiaras for stuffed animals.
Picture frames	I could add wings to the sides of picture frames to make butterfly frames.

WORDS FROM WARREN

The key to success is to be passionate about what you do and to always have a dream.

CHAPTER 2

WHAT CAN I DO?
OFFER A SERVICE

A service business doesn't focus on selling a product. Instead it focuses on doing work for another person or group of people. Taxi drivers, gardeners, barbers, doctors, and lawyers are all in service businesses. Do you have a skill that could be used to help others?

Use What You Know

Starting your own service business can require little or no money and equipment. Service businesses can also offer you a wonderful way to earn money for doing the things you love to do.

When **Noa Mintz** was 12 years old, her mother needed a new babysitter for Noa and her three siblings. Noa had already had lots of babysitters. She'd learned a lot about what made a babysitter great and not so great, so her mom challenged her to find the perfect sitter. The family quickly found out that Noa had a knack for picking out good babysitters and nannies. They also found out that Noa's mother's friends needed her services as well. Noa would interview the sitters, check their references, and match them to the right families. Within a year, she had 50 clients. Two years later, she had an office and an employee handling the day-to-day operations of Nannies by Noa. By then, she had 190 clients! Noa found success when she matched one of her talents to a need in her own New York City community.

Juliette Brindak knows something about how tough it is to be a tween girl. She was one not long ago. Girls' bodies are changing, and there are cliques, bullies, and increased workloads to deal with. When her younger sister was getting ready for middle school, Juliette was worried. She felt that there weren't any websites geared to tweens and the problems they face. To fill that gap, Juliette created a website, Miss O and Friends. It features characters she'd created when she was just 10 years old. Juliette's experience as a young woman helped her reach a market she knew a lot about.

At 11 years old, **Ben Towers** was already interested in technology. Then an author friend of the family asked him to design a website to help her sell her books. With the help of some online tutorials, he did it! Next, Ben began offering his services on a freelancing website. As he grew more confident with his skills, he grew his business. He reached out to the tennis club he belonged to and suggested that their website was boring and could use an update. By the time he was 12, he had 25 clients. By 16, he had hundreds of clients—including his old tennis club.

Fourteen-year-old food lover **Remmi Smith** loves to cook. She is also worried about the problem of childhood obesity. She believes that kids need to see that it is fun to cook healthy, inexpensive food. She combined her interests and talents to try to solve a problem, and now she has an impressive career! Remmi began by filming her online cooking show, *Cook Time with Remmi*. Then her show, *The Culinary Kid*, ran for a few years on a local cable network. People started to notice her, and she was picked to be a student representative for a large food service company. That means that she works with the company's chefs to help them come up with healthy recipes that kids will like. She has also written a cookbook and given cooking demonstrations all around the country.

WORDS FROM WARREN

You're not going to run out of storage room in your brain, so take advantage of everything that is of interest.

Noa knew about babysitters, Juliette knew about being a tween, Ben knew about web design, and Remmi knew about cooking. They all turned their interests and talents into successful businesses. What about you? Can you turn your knowledge into a business?

On-the-Job Learning

One of the best parts of running your own business is that you are always learning. At first, Juliette Brindak knew she had a skill—she could create characters that other girls loved. When she decided that Miss O and Friends should be online, she didn't know how to create a blog or a website. She needed to learn about web design, writing, and promotion.

Juliette was 16 years old when she first launched her site. It was a simple web page that offered some games and an advice column written by Juliette. But she kept learning and improving her site. It is bigger and better now, with message boards, quizzes, games, and music. Juliette had a vision, but she didn't let the fact that she couldn't do it all at once stop her. She launched it, mastered more skills, and then grew her blog—and her business—more and more.

By the time Juliette was 21, the site was among the most popular destinations on the web for tween girls. It was valued at $15 million and had evolved into something entirely different—an online community. As Juliette got older, she didn't feel as if she knew exactly what tween girls were interested in anymore. So she started to use polls, quizzes, and user comments to help her keep up to date. This way, the business can change along with girls' interests. And Juliette continues to learn new things along the way.

What Do You Enjoy?

Think about your talents and the things you do best. You might already have a great idea for a business that can provide a service in your community.

Do you like playing with younger kids? Are you very responsible? You might make an ideal babysitter. Consider opening a babysitting service that allows parents to go out for a night on the town or offers after-school help.

Do you have a way with animals? Offer a service that helps people take care of their pets. You could be a dog walker, a cat sitter, a pet groomer, an animal trainer, or a reptile caretaker.

Do you like to garden? Your own weeding and lawn-mowing service could be a great business. Or perhaps you could plant seeds and sell the flowers, herbs, or vegetables that grow.

Are you a math whiz or a talented writer? Can you *parles français?* Or *hablas español?* Get the word out that you are available for tutoring or homework help.

Do you know a lot about a particular topic and like to write? Consider starting a blog about one of your interests. Maybe you could write about local events for kids and sell advertising space to local businesses.

Do you have an eye for photos, layout, and design? You could create custom photo albums for your parents' friends. For a fee, offer to scan all of the photos they have (from before the days of digital cameras and smartphones) too.

Are you concerned about the environment? Do you compost? Ask your neighbors if you can help them by taking their compostable waste off their hands. Pick up their compostable trash every few days for a fee. When your compost is ready, you can sell it back to your neighbors for their yards and plants. If your small business is successful, you can scale up by approaching local restaurants for their food waste.

WORDS FROM WARREN

Do what you love!

Take Your Skills to the Next Level

List your interests and skills in the chart below, then brainstorm some business ideas that use those skills.

INTERESTS AND SKILLS	BUSINESS IDEAS
I like to spend time with animals. I am responsible.	Dog walking, cleaning fish aquariums, bathing and brushing dogs, pet day care
I like to listen to all kinds of music.	DJing at parties, birthdays, cookouts, and events

What Skills Do You Want to Learn?

Like Juliette Brindak, founder of Miss O and Friends, you can always decide to acquire new skills, offer them to your customers, and grow your business. First, think about what you are interested in. Then find a way to offer a service in that area with skills you already have. You can add new skills and services as you go. Here are some examples.

Start a computer business. Lots of people need help setting up email and social media accounts. You could help them do that, while learning more computer programs. As time goes on, you can offer your customers new services. Learn about coding and design, and soon you might add "website design" to your list of services.

Build a pet-care empire. Start with cat sitting or dog walking, then expand to more complex animal care. Read books, take classes, and volunteer with a vet, and maybe you can add basic obedience training or grooming to your skill set. Learn about reptile care and you may be able to offer a reliable reptile-sitting service for vacationing pet owners too.

Grow a green business. Begin with offering basic lawn mowing and weeding. After that, you may choose to become more knowledgeable about gardening and landscaping. Soon you may be able to offer advice on what types of plants should go in different locations and what time of year to plant them.

You'll have more fun, feel more challenged, and grow your business faster if you work on your skills and expand what your business can offer.

WORDS FROM WARREN

The more you learn, the more you'll earn.

Set Your Sights on New Skills

You don't already have to be an expert in something to want to build a business around it. If you have a vision of a business that is needed in your neighborhood or if there are skills you know you'd like to learn, you can work step-by-step to learn what you need to know to make a successful enterprise.

SKILLS I HAVE	SKILLS I'D LIKE TO HAVE	BUSINESSES I'D LIKE TO CREATE
Solid knowledge about using a computer, social media sites, and word processing programs like Microsoft Word, Pages, Google Docs, etc.	Website design	A computer help service where I can eventually offer website design to my customers
Ballet and jazz dance	Tap dance, choreography	An after-school class or club where I teach different kinds of dance to the kids who join

What Does Your Neighborhood Need?

Before settling on a service to offer, you will want to make sure that it will be in demand in your area. If you live in Florida, a snow-shoveling business is unlikely to succeed. And if you live far from your nearest neighbors, it may be difficult to launch a pet-sitting or dog-walking business. Some successful businesspeople started out simply by finding a need and meeting it.

Start thinking about your location and what services are in demand in your neighborhood. Here are some ideas based on location and situation.

Veggie-free zone. Do you live in a community that doesn't offer much fresh produce? Are you far from the nearest farmers' market? Maybe you could work with the farms or distributors in the area to set up a delivery service. You could create a website that offers recipes featuring the veggies in each week's produce delivery.

Whiteout. Some areas of the country get hit with blizzard after blizzard in the winter. Adults don't always have the time to shovel. They also tend to get tired of moving the white stuff week after week. Let the neighbors know that you are available to take over shoveling their driveways. Business may pile up faster than snowflakes in January.

Baby boom. Some neighborhoods seem to be bursting with babies and younger kids. Do you see strollers everywhere? Is the toddler playground always packed? You may live in the perfect place for a babysitting service.

The Internet Is a Community Too

Think of the Internet as one giant neighborhood. Just as your town needs a grocery store, a post office, a pharmacy, a fire station, and other necessary shops and buildings, the Internet should have a website for every common interest.

Farrhad Acidwalla was incredibly interested in planes and how they work. While researching his favorite topic, he noticed that there was not a central database or place online where people like him could read about and share information about planes. So he built an online community devoted to aviation and building model airplanes. A few months later, he sold the business for $1,200.

When brother and sister pair **Catherine** and **Dave Cook** and their family moved to New Jersey, the kids didn't know anyone. The 15- and 16-year-old siblings flipped through their new school's yearbook, hoping to recognize someone or get some clues about the students they might befriend. But the yearbook wasn't very helpful. And there wasn't a website that solved their problem either. They thought they could put the kind of information found in a yearbook online and turn it into a tool for helping people meet new friends. Six years later, they sold their company, myYearbook.com, for an enormous profit. Now it is called MeetMe.com.

Are all of your interests covered by well-written and well-maintained websites? Is there room for another site dedicated to pandas or jump rope tricks or true stories about pirates? Perhaps all of the online communities about your favorite topics are for adults. Maybe creating a one-stop shop for kids or tweens with similar interests is the perfect business for you.

Services Your Neighbors Need

Are there lots of working people in your neighborhood who might need help with leaf raking in the fall? Maybe there are parents who need someone to meet their kids at the bus stop and walk them home after school? Investigating what is in demand can be a great source for business ideas. Make a list of what may be needed in your neighborhood, then come up with a business solution.

MY NEIGHBORHOOD HAS LOTS OF	IT PROBABLY NEEDS
Snow	Snow shoveling
Cyclists	Someone to clean and maintain bikes (tighten bolts, grease the chain, etc.)

WORDS FROM WARREN

Go to bed a little wiser than when you woke up.

CHAPTER 3.

STANDING OUT
FROM THE CROWD

Once you've decided what kind of business you'd like to be in, there are lots of things you can do to make yourself stand out from other companies. These tips will help you start your business off on the right foot.

Finding Your Niche

A **niche** is like a specialty. It's a special little corner of the market. Having a niche means that you offer a product or service that nobody else is offering in quite the same way or in the same location. What made Juliette Brindak's website special was that it was created "by girls for girls." MyYearbook.com was different from other social networks because it was designed for people to meet one another, not for people who already knew one another. Lizzie Marie Likness (below) found her niche making healthy, tasty snacks.

niche
a specialization, or point of difference, that makes a business stand out from other similar businesses

Lizzie Marie Likness was just 2 years old when she started helping her family in the kitchen. Together they made their own delicious, healthy applesauce. When she was 6 years old, Lizzie Marie wanted to take horseback riding lessons, but she needed to earn the money to pay for them herself. She thought about all the things she could do and had an idea! Her parents were always looking for great-tasting snacks that were also healthy. She thought other people might be looking for them too, so she went to work in the kitchen.

Lizzie Marie developed snacks that were both delicious and healthy and started selling them at farmers' markets. Lots of other people were selling baked goods, like cookies and cupcakes. But Lizzie Marie was the only person selling treats that were both sweet and healthy. Pretty soon, Lizzie Marie was known for her healthy baked goods. She created a website called LizzieMarieCuisine.com where she blogs about healthy cooking. She also gives cooking classes and has even appeared on television to talk about healthy eating.

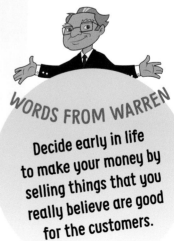

WORDS FROM WARREN

Decide early in life to make your money by selling things that you really believe are good for the customers.

What Makes Your Business Special?

Read the reviews of other similar businesses. See what customers like the most about them. What do customers feel is missing? Is there a particular niche that isn't being filled? What can you do to be different or better?

Wrap it up. Hart Main put his scented candles for men in recycled soup cans. It's memorable, and it makes his candles stand out from the countless other candles on the market. If you are selling bouquets of flowers, try putting them in pretty jars so they are ready to be given as gifts. Put friendship bracelets, headbands, or bow ties in little pouches. Your thoughtful packaging can be your niche.

Take on an extra task. All dog walkers take pooches for walks. But the dog walker who offers to take an unpleasant chore off a dog owner's hands will surely be remembered. Offer to remove any dog poop from your clients' yards. Your clients will certainly appreciate it.

Spice it up. If you have a lemonade stand, offer unique flavors, such as strawberry or blueberry mint.

Turn it inside out. If you have a car-washing business, vacuum the inside of the car and dust the dashboard as well as cleaning the outside. The sparkling car interiors could be the thing that brings your customers back again and again.

Make it personal. Personalizing the items you sell with a customer's name (think pencils, T-shirts, hats) can be a great niche.

What is your niche? How can you make your business memorable?

Present Yourself and Your Business Well

Once you are in business, you will want to think about how your customers see you. Be professional and reliable. Here are a few simple tips for making a good impression on your clients, partners, and your parents (who may be helping you get started).

Be neat and clean. You don't have to dress up to sell lemonade or cookies, but you should realize that appearance makes a difference. Make sure that you and your clothes are always tidy. Nobody wants to buy food from someone with dirty hands!

Keep your work space neat and clean. It's easier to fill an order when you can find where you put it! And harder to be on time if you've misplaced an address or phone number. Having an organized work space will help you find what you need quickly and easily. If you sell food, it's especially important to keep both your cooking and selling spaces clean and organized.

Be kind and understanding. Being nice and friendly will help you create lasting relationships with partners, mentors, clients, and customers. You can turn to your new friends when you need help or advice. And your kindness will mean a lot to your customers. No one wants to do business with a grump!

Build an appealing website or web page. If your business is online, make sure that your page looks fresh and interesting and that the information on your site is clear and easy to read. Dress up your website with color and photographs. Make sure the contact information and order forms are easy to find.

Watch your words. Speak properly and respectfully to everyone. What you say and how you say it reflects on you and your business.

WORDS FROM WARREN

Be careful about how you present yourself. It's not just the outside that counts, it's the whole package.

If your service is outstanding, you'll always stand out.

Concentrate on Customer Service

Learn about your customers and make sure your business is meeting their needs. If you're babysitting, keep notes on what the kids like to do and be prepared to read their favorite books or play their favorite games. Little extras go a long way.

Go the extra mile for your customers to earn their loyalty. If you are weeding a garden, be sure your customer is happy before you leave. Leave flower beds clear of the weeds you pulled and water the flowers if needed. If you are raking leaves, make sure you've gotten them all and bagged them up. Offer to carry the bags to where they should be stored before their pick-up day. If you're babysitting, be sure to put away toys and put any dirty dishes in the dishwasher.

Do your best to anticipate your customers' needs. If you are running a snow-shoveling business, keep track of the weather. If your area is supposed to get several inches of snow, call or email your customers to make a plan even before the storm starts.

If you ever make a mistake or deliver poor service, make up for it immediately. Did you forget to remove the snow from the edge of the driveway? Or block up a storm drain? Go back and complete the job. Did the elastic on a brand-new headband snap? Replace it right away. If you show up late for a babysitting job, don't make excuses—apologize immediately and offer to throw in an hour for free.

Enlist a Mentor

One way to learn more about your business—or a business you *want* to be in—is to speak with someone who is already in that business. A mentor acts like a teacher or a guide. Mentors will share stories about their experiences. They will help you grow, learn, and become better at something. As you start to run your business, share your experiences with your mentors so they can offer advice and point out things you may not have thought of yet.

When 15-year-old **Catherine** and 16-year-old **Dave Cook** founded their social networking site for teens, myYearbook.com, they didn't need to look far for a mentor. Their older brother, Geoff, had already launched and sold a start-up company. The siblings had all grown up together. Catherine and Dave knew they shared the same values as Geoff. And they knew immediately that Geoff was the one to go to for business advice.

To get her Love Sandal ready for the marketplace, **Abi Smithson** worked with an organization that helps entrepreneurs by putting them in touch with mentors. One of her mentors was Robert Ott, head of the fashion department at a nearby university. He was impressed with Abi's creativity and her design idea. She knew exactly what her product should look like and who she was selling to. Robert worked with Abi to develop her brand, improve her business plan, and find the right materials for her sandals.

WORDS FROM WARREN

The best thing I did was to choose the right heroes.

Practice, Practice, Practice

Studying every day will help you get smarter, and exercising every day will help you stay healthy. It is also important to stay disciplined in business. Try to do little things right every day. Don't cut corners—even when you are tired. Your commitment to good habits will help you succeed in business.

Team Up

Lots of things are more fun if you do them with a friend or family member. Business is no exception. And, often, two people can come up with more great ideas than one.

Lutece Kramer-Guillemot and **Tess Olmi**, best friends and neighbors in Brooklyn, New York, started their business, Marbelous, when they were just 8 years old. They designed and made beautiful handmade clay beads, which they hung from pretty silk cords to make necklaces. With help from their moms, they got some boutiques to carry the necklaces, and word spread quickly.

Having partners can also be a big help in splitting up the workload.

Lily, Chloe, and **Sophie Warren** are the Sweet Bee Sisters. They were 9, 7, and 5 when they came up with the idea to make lip balm using beeswax leftover from their parents' beehives. The sisters researched and planned the business together, but each has her own area of expertise. Lily reads and responds to all of the emails and fills the orders the company receives. Chloe is in charge of the recipes. She makes most of the product (with help from her sisters if she needs it). And Sophie helps with packing up and labeling the product.

WORDS FROM WARREN

Great partnerships will make any job easier.

Do you have a friend you like to make things with? Do you know someone who is a great salesperson? Someone who has a gift for growing plants? Or is a terrific cook? Is there someone in your life who is really good at the things that you're not as good at, and vice versa? That person may make a great business partner!

CHAPTER 4

THE MONEY PART

Some businesses—like **manufacturing** businesses—need a lot of money to get started because of the cost of equipment and materials. Others, such as a babysitting service, require little or no money up front. But all entrepreneurs need to know how money works. It's important to tally up all of your expenses, to understand how to calculate your profits (all the money you'll be making), to know when you will **break even**, and to set a price for your goods and services. You may also need ideas for raising money.

Start-Up Costs vs. Operating Costs

There are two main types of costs to consider when starting a business: start-up costs and operating costs.

Start-up costs are generally one-time costs. Operating costs are ongoing. If you're washing cars, your start-up costs will include the cost of buckets, sponges, and a hose. Your operating costs will include the cost of cleaning products and marketing materials.

Before starting your cookie business, you will need to make sure you have an oven, a refrigerator, and all of the bowls, mixers, baking sheets, spatulas, cookie cutters, spoons, and other utensils you need to store ingredients and bake cookies. Do you decorate the cookies? You may need to buy a reusable decorating bag and decorating tips. Lucky for you, you can probably use the refrigerator and oven that are already in your home, along with your parents' cooking supplies. That will help keep your start-up costs low.

See what you can borrow to get your business started. Once your business is going well, you can think about returning the borrowed items and buying your own. Be resourceful.

Jake and **Lachlan Johnson**, of Beaux Up, save money on their operating costs by using the material from vintage neckties to make bow ties.

manufacturing
making products. It usually refers to making things on a large scale, using machinery.

break even
when you reach the point that your earnings cover your costs

WORDS FROM WARREN

Rule #1: Never lose money.
Rule #2: Never forget rule #1.

37

What Are Your Start-Up Costs?

Write down all the things you will need to get your business started and how much they cost. Add them together. These are your start-up costs.

ITEMS NEEDED TO START A BUSINESS	COST
	$
	$
	$
	$
	$
	$
	$
	$
	$
	$
	$
TOTAL	$

Use Your Savings

Do you get money for your birthday and other holidays? How about an allowance? Instead of spending it, save some or all of it.

When **Katelyn Lohr** decided to start her toeless socks business, she was able to do it without asking her parents for money. She used saved-up birthday money to buy her first batch of socks.

Start a Starter Business

Even if you have big ideas, you may have to start small to raise the money you need for a more costly business. If you dream of having a landscaping business, you may have to weed a few small gardens first to build up your savings.

Cameron Johnson didn't spend the money he made in his first business (creating and selling greeting cards). He used it to start another business reselling Beanie Babies. What happened next? You may have guessed it already. Cameron didn't blow his earnings. He created more businesses.

Campaign for the Money

One way to raise money without taking out a loan is to use a site like Piggybackr.com or KidBacker.com. Using text, photos, and video, you create a campaign that spells out your vision for your company or product. You explain how much money you need, why you want it, and what the money will be used for. Then you share your campaign with friends, family, and anyone who might be interested in making a donation.

Raising money in this way is called **crowdfunding**. If your campaign is successful, you will end up with the start-up money you need, and you will have already started spreading the word about your company.

Make sure to talk to your parents before considering a crowdfunding campaign. Depending on your age and the site you choose, your parents may need to be involved in the campaign. Also make sure to read all of the rules of a site before you use it. Some crowdfunding sites require you to set all-or-nothing goals. That means that if you set up a campaign with a goal of raising $450, then you will need to raise $450 or more in order to receive anything. If you only raise $300, then you will not receive any money at all.

Fourteen-year-old **Erik Meike**, 13-year-old **Briana Das**, 11-year-old **Leona Das**, and 11-year-old **Elise Meike** were interested in a type of soil-free gardening called aeroponics, where plants are grown in air using a fogging machine. Using Piggybackr.com, they raised $1,130 (more than their goal of $945) to improve the design of their aeroponic system. Some of the funds they raised went to purchasing supplies so they could lower the cost of the aeroponics workshops they teach. Three years later, this clever and creative foursome is still working. They go by the name Tribe Awesome, and their goal is "to help people find their inner awesomeness and make what matters."

KidBacker.com was actually founded by a young entrepreneur, 9-year-old **Carly Holst-Knudsen**. And how did she raise the start-up funds she needed? With her parents' help, Carly raised the money using GoFundMe.com, a crowdfunding site that is aimed at adults.

crowdfunding
raising the money for a project by getting donations (often small donations) from a large number of people

WORDS FROM WARREN

Any course can be exciting. Mastering accounting is like mastering a new language, it can be so much fun.

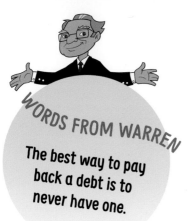

Borrow the Money

It's easy to get into trouble by borrowing money, so think hard about whether a loan makes sense for you. Before you try to get a loan from an adult (or a bank), you will need to get prepared. Draw up a business plan (see Chapter 8) and rehearse your elevator pitch (see Chapter 6). Decide up front how much you need to borrow, when you're going to pay back the money, and what you will give up if, for any reason, you're not able to pay it back.

Farrhad Acidwalla was only 13 years old when he decided to borrow the smallest amount possible to get his business going. He asked his parents for $10 to purchase a domain name so he could start his website. He identified the need for an online community devoted to discussing airplanes and model airplanes. Then he borrowed a small but necessary amount of money and built his site. In just a few months, he sold the business for $1,200.

After using a chemical hair relaxer that left her nearly bald at 11, **Jasmine Lawrence** dedicated her time to making natural hair products. At 13, she attended a summer camp to learn more about starting her own business. Then she asked her parents for a loan. Her parents noted that Jasmine had put in the time at business camp. That showed them how serious she was. And she had some money saved up from her allowance. If the business did not take off, Jasmine promised to give her parents all of her saved-up allowance money and to work off her debt doing chores. Her parents agreed to a $2,000 loan, and EDEN BodyWorks was born. Now her products are found in Target, Walmart, CVS, and other major retailers around the country.

What Are Your Operating Costs?

Operating costs are all of the day-to-day costs you will have when running your business. If you make beads for jewelry, you will need to keep buying clay. If you're selling cookies, then your operating costs will include all of the ingredients you use and any packaging you need to provide. A lawn-mowing business won't have many operating costs. You will need gas for the mower. And you may choose to spend money to print flyers or run an ad in your local paper.

Write down all of the day-to-day costs of your business (or what you think they will be).

SUPPLIES NEEDED TO KEEP THE BUSINESS RUNNING	COSTS
	$
	$
	$
	$
	$
	$
	$
	$
	$
	$
	$
	$
	$
TOTAL	$

Calculate Your Profit

You should calculate your potential profit before you even get started. This will help you determine what to charge for your product or service. It will help you know much you can spend. Knowing how much money you may be able to earn can tell you if your idea is a good one. It can also help you think of ways to increase your profit.

STEP 1: Determine Your Cost per Unit

Take all your operating expenses and add them together. Then divide the total of your expenses by the number of items (or units) you made.

For this example, we'll look at a lemonade stand. Below are the ingredients (lemons and sugar) and supplies (cups) you will need to make 2 gallons of lemonade. Each 2-gallon batch yields 20 cups of lemonade.

ITEMS NEEDED TO RUN A LEMONADE STAND (along with some math to figure out how much the items cost)	COST
Juice from 20 lemons Each lemon is $0.50. $0.50 x 20 lemons = $10	$10
2 cups of sugar A 5-pound bag of sugar is about $5.50. There are about 11 cups of sugar in every 5-pound bag. $5.50 ÷ 11 = $0.50 That means each cup of sugar costs 50 cents. $0.50 x 2 = $1	$1
20 plastic cups for serving A bag of 60 cups is $3. $3 ÷ 60 = $0.05. That means each cup costs 5 cents. $0.05 x 20 = $1	$1
TOTAL	$12

It will cost $12 just to make 2 gallons (20 cups) of lemonade. To find out how much it costs per cup, divide the total cost ($12) by the number of cups made (20). The cost per cup is $0.60.

Total Cost		Number of Units		Cost per Unit
$12.00	÷	20	=	$0.60

Step 2: Determine a Selling Price and Calculate Your Profit

What would happen if you sold each cup of lemonade for $0.50? Let's find out.

Figure out your profit (or loss) by taking the selling price of your product ($0.50) and subtracting your cost per unit ($0.60).

Selling Price		Cost per Unit		Profit per Unit
$0.50	-	$0.60	=	- $0.10

That's a loss of 10 cents for each cup of lemonade you sell! You would have to raise your prices—or reduce your costs—if you wanted to make a profit.

Let's try this again. This time, let's raise the cost of your product to $1 for every cup sold.

Selling Price		Cost per Unit		Profit per Unit
$1.00	-	$0.60	=	$0.40

That's better! That yields a profit of $0.40 on every cup!

What happens if you raise the cost of a cup of lemonade to $2?

Selling Price		Cost per Unit		Profit per Unit
$2.00	-	$0.60	=	$1.40

Wow! $1.40 profit per cup is great!

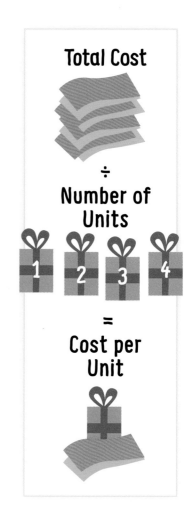

Total Cost

÷

Number of Units

1 2 3 4

=

Cost per Unit

WORDS FROM WARREN

Price is what you pay, value is what you get.

Supply and Demand

Supply and demand are two important forces in business. *Supply* refers to how much of something there is. *Demand* refers to how much of something people want. Understanding supply and demand is important in business because it can help to determine how much a customer will pay for a product and how much you should charge for it.

If a business makes too much of a product (or that product is not selling quickly), there will be too much supply. If a company has not produced enough of a product, the supply will be low. When lots of people want a product, there is a high demand for it. When only a small number of people want a certain product, there is low demand for the item.

How does this relate to price? If there is more of an item than people need, prices will fall. But when demand is high and supply is low, a consumer might pay a high price to get their hands on what they want.

Cameron Johnson (who had some money set aside from his first business, making and selling cards) used his knowledge of supply and demand to start a second business, reselling Beanie Babies. He noticed stores were selling out of the popular stuffed animals. He also noticed that, among kids his sister's age, the demand for Beanie Babies was huge. The supply just couldn't keep up. So he offered his younger sister $100 for her collection of Beanie Babies. She accepted. Cameron then resold the dolls on eBay for much more than they were sold in stores. With the money he made, Cameron bought more dolls at wholesale prices. Cameron resold the dolls on his company website and on eBay. Within one year, Cameron had banked $50,000.

wholesale

the sale of goods in large quantities, often for a lower cost. Retailers usually buy in bulk, at **wholesale** prices, and then resell at a profit.

How Much Is Too Much?

Selling cups of lemonade at $2 per cup means that you make a profit of $1.40 per cup. You could make even more money if you raised the price to $3. But the question is, should you? Your potential customers may think $3 is just too expensive for a cup of lemonade. They may walk away when they learn the price, and then you won't make any profit at all.

WORDS FROM WARREN

No business can grow and be successful if you spend your money as fast as you make it. And even if you only save a little bit, over time it will grow and grow, and soon you'll be able to buy as many video games as you want!

Accepting Money

If you are setting up a table on your corner, at the local pool, or at a craft fair, be prepared to accept cash from your customers. Make sure you have extra bills and coins to make change. A bank or local restaurant will usually be happy to trade a $20 bill for some $1s and $5s (or whatever kind of change you need).

Using a credit card reader, like Square, will allow you to take credit card payments. That can open up your sales to an even bigger market! Your parent or guardian will need to download the free Square app and set up a Square account. Then you can plug the Square Reader into a smartphone or tablet and start taking payments.

The Right Price

Price is a big part of what makes people buy or not buy a product. At 50 cents per cup, you may sell lots of lemonade, but you'd be taking a loss on every cup. That's no way to run a business. At $1 per cup, you're making a small profit. At $2 a cup, you've got a nice-sized profit—but you may risk losing some customers who don't want to spend that much on a cup of lemonade.

Figuring out what to charge for your products and services can be one of the most difficult parts of being an entrepreneur. You want to make a fair profit, but you also want to be sure that you are delivering good value for your customers. Here are some tips for settling on the right price.

Crunch the numbers. Figure out your costs. Be sure that you're selling your product for more than it costs you to produce. If you are selling a service such as dog walking, babysitting, or giving guitar lessons, think about what your time is worth (for more on your hourly wage, see page 94).

Check out the competition. Ask around and look at websites and ads to see what similar businesses are charging. If most babysitters in your town are charging $12 an hour and you are priced at $8 an hour, you may be underpricing your services. But consider factors such as experience level. If you are new to the business, you may have to charge a bit less for a while until you build your reputation.

Be creative. You don't have to charge the same amount every time. Reward loyal customers by giving them a price break, discount, or even a freebie—like a free banana or muffin with a cup of lemonade— every now and then. Snag new customers with an introductory price. Hold an opening-day promotion to get those sales rolling. Or offer a free hour of babysitting when someone hires you for the first time.

WORDS FROM WARREN

Learn from your mistakes— better yet, learn from the mistakes of others.

What Is Your "Break-Even?"

When a business makes enough money through sales to cover all of the costs of the business (including start-up costs), the company has reached its "break-even point," or break-even. Only when the company has passed the break-even point can it be considered profitable.

Calculating your break-even point takes some math. To find the break-even for a lemonade stand, let's figure out the business's start-up costs. These include a pitcher, a tablecloth, and some poster board. Let's assume you were able to borrow a large wooden spoon, measuring cups, a folding table and chairs, and some markers (to make a sign) from your parents.

Start with the Start-Up Costs!
Add up the costs of the things you had to buy to get started.

Start-Up Needs	Cost
2-gallon pitcher for making and serving lemonade	$15
1 tablecloth	$3
Poster board for sign	$2
Borrowed spoon, measuring cups, card table, chairs, and markers	Free
TOTAL START-UP COSTS	$20

Calculating Your Break-Even
Let's say you priced the lemonade at $1 per cup so the profit from this business is $0.40 per cup of lemonade sold. How many cups of lemonade would

Total Start-Up Costs

$20

÷

Profit per Unit

$0.40

=

Break-Even
50 cups

your business have to sell to cover the $20 of start-up costs? Divide your total start-up costs by the profit made on every cup of lemonade you sell.

Total Start-Up Costs		Profit per Unit		Number of Units to Sell to Reach the Break-Even
$20	÷	$0.40	=	50

You would have to sell 50 cups of lemonade before your business would be profitable.

When Will You Break Even?

How long would it take you to sell 50 cups of lemonade? Here's where you'll have to do some guesswork. But you'll want to come up with a realistic estimate. If you are selling lemonade outside of a ball field where kids will be practicing every day after school, think of how busy the location is and how many thirsty parents and kids will be around. Surely you can sell 10 cups of lemonade each day. How about 20? 25? If you think you can sell 25 cups of lemonade a day, how many days will it take for you to break even? Divide the number of units (cups) that need to be sold to reach the break-even point by the number of units sold per day.

Number of Units to Sell to Reach the Break-Even		Number of Units Sold per Day		Days to Break-Even
50	÷	25	=	2

If your lemonade stand succeeded in selling 25 cups of lemonade per day, you would earn back your start-up costs and break even after two days.

Only 2 days to break-even!

CHAPTER 5

LOCATION, LOCATION, LOCATION

It has been said that a business's top three decisions are location, location, location. Big stores do a lot of research before they open a new location. And so should you.

Where Should You Set Up Shop?

What kind of neighborhood do you live in? Who lives there? Which nearby stores, businesses, and parks are busy?

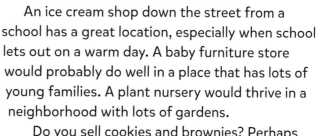

An ice cream shop down the street from a school has a great location, especially when school lets out on a warm day. A baby furniture store would probably do well in a place that has lots of young families. A plant nursery would thrive in a neighborhood with lots of gardens.

Do you sell cookies and brownies? Perhaps you could set up shop near a pizza place that doesn't have dessert on the menu. Do you sew scarves using cool, retro fabrics? Maybe you should set up a stand near an outdoor music venue or near the local library. If cheerleading practice, band practice, the conservation club, and play rehearsal all let out at around the same time, that might be the perfect time to show off your products in front of school (as long as your school officials do not object). Are your products perfect for summertime? Set up a table outside the town pool.

Go Where Your Customers Are

Ray Kroc, the founder of McDonald's, used to say, "I'm not in the burger business, I'm in the real estate business." Ray knew that finding a good location to sell his hamburgers was very important. Many McDonald's and other fast-food restaurants are directly off highways, making them easy for truck drivers and travelers to spot. The customers literally roll in.

Pair Up Products and Places

We've listed some types of businesses below, along with some areas where a business might thrive. Can you match the business to a good location? There are no right or wrong answers, but think about how each particular business might work in each one of these spots.

Lawn-mowing/gardening business	A small town with lots of young families, little kids, and babies
A food cart that sells hot dogs, lemonade, and snacks	A suburban neighborhood with lots of lawns and lots of people who like to relax on weekends
Used books for sale	A busy park or sports field with lots of people, families, and kids
Babysitting business	A school playground just as school lets out
Handmade friendship bracelets	The stoop of an apartment building in the city

Where Does Your Business Belong?

Now brainstorm some good locations for your business. And think of some locations you might want to avoid.

YOUR BUSINESS NAME	POSSIBLE LOCATIONS FOR YOUR BUSINESS	LOCATIONS THAT WON'T WORK FOR YOUR BUSINESS

Get Moving

Think about your business. Do you sell snacks, lemonade, or ice cream sandwiches? It might be worth it to take your business on the road in a wagon or cart. Then you could move from one busy ball field to another. (Just be sure to check local rules first—some communities require permits.)

For **Jaden Wheeler** and **Amaya Selmon**, many locations were a better option than a single great location. They are a brother-sister team who started selling snow cones in their front yard when they were 10 and 12 years old. They worked so hard developing tasty recipes and attracting customers to their yard—and made so much money—that their mom decided to invest in a truck so they could make their business mobile. Then their mom drove the Kool Kidz Sno Konez truck around town on weekends while the duo mixed up flavors like *Go Bananas!, Pow Pina Colada, I <3 Pink Lemonade,* and *OMG Orange*. Having a truck allowed them to always be in the right place at the right time and to relocate easily if an area got too quiet.

Cory Nieves wanted to buy a car for his mother when he was just 5 years old. He started selling hot cocoa to earn money. Pretty soon, he was selling cookies too. His sweets became really popular, so he launched Mr. Cory's Cookies. On weekends, Cory loads up a wagon with his cookies and walks around his neighborhood, selling his sweets for $1. Since his "shop" is on wheels, it is easy for Cory to take his goods from a barbershop to a car dealership and then to a special event. By making his local business a mobile business, he can sell 1,000 cookies in a weekend.

Selling Online

Before you set up an online shop for your products, spend some time thinking about your favorite online stores. What do you like about them? Why do you return to them again and again? Think about the items you buy online. What have you purchased online? Are there types of things that you would never search for online?

Are you selling used books? Hand-painted skateboards? Knit hats? T-shirts? Soaps in the shape of cartoon characters? Whatever you've decided to sell, there can be an online storefront for you. A virtual store enables you to sell your products to people all over the country without ever leaving your home. You just need to remember to charge a fee for the packing and shipping of your product.

Setting Up Shop

Some people set up their own websites to sell things, but lots of people use a third-party service to help. Sites like Amazon.com, eBay.com, and Etsy.com are all sites to look at if you want to become an online seller.

Etsy.com is a site geared toward people selling handmade goods, and it was the perfect fit for **Kia'i Tallett.** When Kia'i was just 5 years old, she began to knit—and she never stopped. By the time she was 11, Kia'i had an Etsy shop called Pixsea Handmade where she sold hand-knit hats, felted flowers, and crocheted items. Her father makes rings using leftover resin from his surfboard-shaping business, and Kia'i helps to make and sell those too.

For **Gabrielle Jordan,** creating a website for her company wasn't the right choice at first. Gabrielle started crafting jewelry and selling her handmade designs to friends and family at the age of 7. In 2009, at the age of 9, she founded her company, Jewelz of Jordan, and began selling her wares at local seminars and workshops. In 2011, the business was ready to reach a wider audience, so she launched her online store.

Some entrepreneurs, like Moziah Bridges of Mo's Bows, start out using a third-party shop (he used Etsy) and then eventually create their own website.

Where to Sell Services

You can also provide services online. Website building, blog writing, graphic design, and tutoring (via Skype or email) can all be offered, delivered, and paid for online. Just like selling products, you can sell your services on your own website. But it's often easier to do it through a site that is already set up, like Fiverr.com.

One young entrepreneur who succeeded in building an online service business is **Ashley Qualls.** She was only 14 when she began creating patterns and layouts for people's pages on MySpace, an early social networking site. She gave away her designs for free. But her site was so popular that she was able to earn money by selling ads on her site. She also tutored other kids, helping them with graphic design and coding. At one point, her website, WhateverLife.com, was getting more than 7 million viewers a month. Ashley set up shop online, which is exactly where her customers are.

WORDS FROM WARREN

Location is very important. It is a vital part of most businesses.

CHAPTER 6

YOU ARE YOUR BRAND

What is a brand? It is a group of goods that have the same name and are made by the same company. For example, Coca-Cola is one brand of soda. Nike, Adidas, and Converse are all brands of sneakers. Over the years, branding has come to mean much more than that. Manufacturers and marketers use the term "brand" to refer to all of the characteristics that people think of when they think of a particular brand.

logo

the symbol that represents a brand

tagline

a short phrase that reflects the personality and/or mission of a business, and often accompanies a brand and logo. It may appear on a company's website, product labels, and other packaging.

slogan

a catchy phrase that describes or helps sell a product

WORDS FROM WARREN

Your premium brand had better be delivering something special, otherwise, you won't get the business.

Branding 101

Branding is important to any business. It says who you are, what you offer, and what you stand for. Customers choose one brand over another because of what that brand represents (such as fun, quality, or value) and because they know what they can expect when they do business with a particular brand. *Your* brand is just as important.

The way you present yourself and your business is part of your brand. Do you want to be seen as trustworthy and reliable? As hip and fashionable? As always up to date and knowledgeable about technology? These are attributes you can convey with your actions as well as with your company name, colors, logo, tagline, or slogans.

How to Build Your Brand

Your brand represents you and your company and tells customers what they can expect when they do business with you. At the core of branding is trust. Your brand is your reputation. Take care in building it and maintaining it.

Here are some of the characteristics you might want to get across to your customers.

→ You will follow through with any promises you make.

→ You will provide a good product.

→ You will provide a consistent product. For example, if you are baking and selling muffins, those muffins will be the same size and shape each time. Each batch will taste the same.

→ You are reliable.

→ You will show up when you are supposed to.

→ You will complete your work on time.

→ You will bring all of your supplies with you to complete your job.

→ You are fair.

→ You are pleasant to work with.

Making these characteristics part of your brand will help customers trust you and respect you and your business. They will return to you again and again.

Beyond trust, what is involved in building a brand? Let's take a look.

WORDS FROM WARREN

Protect your reputation. It takes years to build a reputation but only minutes to ruin it.

Brand Loyalty

When you try on new sneakers, do you always look for the same brand? When your parents buy groceries, do they always buy the same brand of orange juice or ketchup or macaroni and cheese? If the answer to any of these questions is yes, then you or your parents are displaying a loyalty to a brand. Think about why you choose to buy these products or services over competitors'. Talk to your parents about services they have used in the past, such as painters, movers, or mechanics. Which of these people or companies have they used more than once? Why? Which of these people or companies did they (or would they) avoid using again. Why?

Think about some brands you like. Do you drink Honest Tea because it is made with natural ingredients? Do you like Air Jordan sneakers because they're cool? Do you use only Wilson tennis racquets because you think they give you better control of the ball? What do you want people to think about when they think of you and your business? The answer will help you as you brand your business.

What's Your Mission?

Think for a moment about your product or service and what you aim to do with it. Who are you making it for and why? Now try to put it into words. This is your mission. Here are two examples from the winners of the Warren Buffett's Secret Millionaires Club "Grow Your Own Business Challenge."

Shine So Bright. When **Aria Eppinger** pitched her business idea, Shine So Bright, during the "Grow Your Own Business Challenge" in 2012, she stated her goals clearly. "I wanted a quick and easy way to make a beautiful light-up design on any piece of clothing. Shine So Bright will sell a kit that contains LEDs, colored conductive thread, switches, and batteries through an online website." She described her customers as "people who want to have bright, cheery clothes that are easy and inexpensive. Shine So Bright is a great family activity, and can be done in social groups such as Girl Scouts and parties."

WiseGuide. Krystal and **Allyson Graylin** and **Kei Chua** had the winning team entry in the "Grow Your Own Business Challenge" in 2014. They also stated the mission for their business clearly: "WiseGuide is an online community that connects people of all ages. The problem today is that kids are spending less time with their grandparents and the elderly. We wanted to share the opportunity to connect with grandparents and the elderly no matter the distance. From personal experience, we know that the elderly have many things to teach, and we also have things that we can share. WiseGuide users can post stories, how-to's, quotes, videos, advice and more. People can also answer questions or requests that have been posted. Our main goal is to help people, while money making is secondary."

What's in a Name?

Choosing a name for your company or product is fun, but it can be tough to find just the right one. You want it to match your business and be memorable. When you are thinking of names, say them out loud. Make sure your name is easy to pronounce and spelled in a way that anyone can read it and get it right. Is it short and sweet and fun to say? Try it out on your siblings and friends. Do they get it? Do a search online to make sure no one in your area has the same name.

    If your company's name is several words long, you may find yourself referring to it by its initials, or its **acronym**. Make sure the acronym of your company's name doesn't spell out anything silly.

acronym

an abbreviation formed from the initial letters of a group of words. For example, the **acronym** for the National Aeronautics and Space Administration is NASA. The **acronym** for the Hewlett-Packard is HP.

Choose Your Colors

Once you have chosen a name, think about the colors that work best for your company. Choose two or three that look nice together. If you make jewelry using shells, think about using colors inspired by the beach, such as blue, green, and sandy beige. FishFlops is a line of flip-flops featuring beachy designs created by kid entrepreneur Madison Nicole Robinson. The branding for FishFlops uses a sunshiny orange and a bright blue.

    Juliette Brindak chose shades of purple and a rich hot pink for the coloring of Miss O and Friends. The Sweet Bee Sisters went with gold and green. The KidBacker.com colors are a crisp green and cool gray, along with black and white.

    Use your brand colors in your logo and on your packaging. Are you selling lemonade? Try selling it in cups in your company's brand colors. Want people to remember your branding? Wear a T-shirt in your company colors when you sell at the local farmers' market.

Which Logos Catch Your Eye?

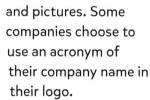

Once you've figured out your company's mission, its name, and the colors that represent it, it's time to design a logo. This may be words or a graphic (or both) that represent your company.

Can you think of any famous logos? Maybe you know, off the top of your head, what the Disney logo looks like. How about Nickelodeon? McDonald's? Target? Apple? When you see the bright orange Nickelodeon logo, you instantly know that the show you are watching is going to be playful and fun. The golden *M* on the red background that makes up the McDonald's logo really stands out. You can see it in the distance on a road trip and know instantly that burgers and fries are not far away. The red bull's-eye of the Target logo is bold and recognizable too.

The next time you are shopping or out in the car, do some logo spotting. Take pictures when you see them or sketch them for reference later. You will notice that some logos are symbols, some logos are simply made up of the company's name, and some logos are made up of a combination of words and pictures. Some companies choose to use an acronym of their company name in their logo.

What makes memorable logos stand out?

What Do Logos Say to You?

After you've spent some time looking at logos, try to put into words what the logo conveys to you. Does a food company's logo give you a clue about whether the food is spicy or sweet? Does a clothing company's logo tell you whether they make clothes for kids or adults? Look at the shape and color of the letters in a logo. Would you describe it as bold and fearless? Refreshing? Soothing? Fun? Welcoming? Elegant? Goofy? Old-fashioned? There are no right or wrong answers here, and it is okay if some logos don't grab your attention at all.

COMPANY NAME	WHAT DOES THEIR LOGO SAY TO YOU?

Make Your Own Logo

Big companies hire branding experts and logo designers to create one-of-a-kind logos. But if you run a small business, you might design your own.

Start sketching. Think of an image or several images that represent your brand personality or give hints about your product or mission. Incorporate your company's colors into the images. Include your brand's name. Sketch. Be creative. Be unique. The FishFlops logo contains the company name with a colorful drawing of a fish. The logo is fun, bright, and summery. And it matches the personality of the company and the flip-flops it makes. The Beaux Up logo features the company name, with the letter *X* "wearing" a striped bow tie. With one look at the logo, you can guess the company makes and sells bow ties.

Use your words. Try making an image part of your company's name. For the Sweet Bee Sisters logo, the cute stylized image of a honeybee forms the *B* in "Bee." In the Mr. Cory's Cookies logo, the *O* is a cookie—a cookie wearing glasses, just like the real-life Cory. Try a version of your logo where you use letters only. See if you like that better. The logo for Marbelous is the company name in a sophisticated script font, perfect for the elegant handmade bead business.

Draw, write, or type. You can use a computer drawing program or draw your logo by hand. If you don't like to draw, enlist the help of an artsy friend or family member.

Take your time. It's okay if you don't like the first few logos you draw. Take your time to find a logo you like since it will be on your website, packaging, business cards, and more.

Make it digital. Use a scanner to scan your logo. Or take a photo of it with a cell phone or digital camera. Then upload your logo to a computer.

Put it to work. Use your logo to make business cards and to add flair to your social media. Print your logo on sticker sheets. If you are selling merchandise online, use the stickers on your packaging or mailing labels so your customers know they are receiving a special product in the mail.

Wanted: Taglines and Slogans that Say It All

Taglines and slogans tell people, in clever and memorable ways, what a business or product is about. Taglines tell something about the business, and slogans tell something about a product. They are used on business cards, websites, social media, and advertising.

Mikaila Ulmer was only 4 years old when she began making and selling her own lemonade sweetened with local honey. As part of her mission, she donates time and money to keep honeybees safe and healthy. Her tagline for BeeSweet Lemonade references her commitment to help the bees: "Buy a Bottle . . . Save a Bee."

Jake and **Lachlan Johnson's** mix-and-match two-piece bow-tie business is committed to providing new, cooler bow-tie looks to young men. They chose "Redefining the Gentleman" as the tagline for their business.

When **Lyla Black** was 3 years old, she drew a little monster figure. She said she wanted to get a monster for her father to keep other monsters from bothering him while he slept. Then she and her mom sewed a fabric version of the monster. A year later, Lyla and her mom began selling their homemade monsters at a local craft fair. Now Lyla is 8, and the monster business is booming. She named her business Lyla Tov, which means "good night" in Hebrew, and her slogan is "Lyla Tov Monsters—for a good night's sleep."

Nine-year-old **Alina Morse** was running errands with her dad one day when a bank teller offered her a lollipop. But Alina knew that eating sugar was bad for her teeth. On the car ride home, she asked her father if they could make lollipops that were actually good for teeth. They did research, talked to dentists, taste-tested a lot of healthy candy, and created Zollipops. The Zollipops logo is in the same bright colors as the sweets, and the Os look like lollipops. Their tagline, "The clean teeth pops," makes their mission clear in just four words.

In her research, Alina found out that tooth enamel is softer for a little while after you eat because your mouth becomes more acidic when you chew. There is an ingredient in Zollipops that helps to neutralize the acidity. So she says that eating a Zollipop right after a meal is a great plan. To get this idea out there, they use the slogan "The After You Eat Treat."

David Eilers started his lawn-mowing business at 10 years old. By 15, he had three trucks, two employees, and lots of equipment, and he was making nearly $50,000 a year. He credits his brother with the simple tagline that helped him get his business going: "David's Mowing Service: We Can Cut It."

Your Perfect Pitch

Imagine you need a loan to get your business off the ground, and you find yourself in an elevator with the ideal investor. You'll want to get your point across, quickly and clearly—in the time it takes to get to your floor. **"Elevator pitch"** is a business term. It is a short description of your business or product designed to get others interested in your business.

Can you sum up your business—and what makes it special—in three or four sentences? Once you've got the perfect pitch, write it down, and practice it out loud. Then, try it in front of an audience. You might convince somebody (maybe mom or dad, or grandma or grandpa) to become an investor!

Match the Taglines

Some company names and taglines are filled in below. What do the taglines tell you about each business? What do you like or not like about them? Pay attention to other company taglines and fill more in as you notice them. Which ones are memorable?

COMPANY	TAGLINE	DO YOU LIKE THIS TAGLINE? WHY OR WHY NOT?
Dunkin' Donuts	*America Runs on Dunkin'*	
Lay's Potato Chips	*Betcha Can't Eat Just One*	
Disneyland	*The Happiest Place on Earth*	
Nike	*Just Do It.*	

WORDS FROM WARREN

Find your passion.

Write Your Own!

Creating a tagline or slogan is a great exercise for a business owner. It makes you think about the essence of your business and what your company represents. Can you come up with a tagline for your business? Or a slogan for your product? Think about what is fun and special about your business. Start by just writing down words that describe your brand. What do you want to get across right away?

All your branding—logo, taglines, colors, and packaging—should reflect the very special personality of your business.

WORDS FROM WARREN

Every business needs to promote itself to sell products and to distinguish itself from the competition.

CHAPTER 7

MARKETING

Once you have a great idea for a business and you've spent some time creating the branding that best represents your company, what's next? It's time to spread the word. The more people who hear about your amazing products or your much-needed service, the more potential customers you have. That's where marketing comes in.

Reaching Your Market

You will need to identify a target market—those are the people who are most likely to be interested in your goods or services. Then you will need to let those people know about you and your incredible business.

Charles Cheng, Lucien Mount, Alejandro Astudillo, and **Nataniel Natanov** formed the winning team in the 1st Annual Warren Buffett's Secret Millionaires Club "Grow Your Own Business Challenge." They got their idea for Deals on Wheels when they needed to raise money for their school. Deals on Wheels would be a portable school store on wheels. Their target market was made up of principals and parents associations. The boys explained: "These customers would purchase the Deals on Wheels cart and merchandise to fill the portable store. Our secondary target group is the students and faculty that would buy the supplies that the principal and the parents association purchased from Deals on Wheels." The principal at the boys' school was their first investor!

How Do You Find a Great Business?

To answer this question, think about where you find out about the latest video game or the scooter you want to buy. Do you notice what your friends have? Do you pay attention to commercials? Do you let your parents pick based on price? Talk to your parents, grandparents, aunts, and uncles. How do they decide which restaurants to go to, what clothing to buy, and which events to attend? Ask the people you know how they hear about the things they buy and the services they use.

Get Them Talking!

Word-of-mouth marketing is when customers talk about a product or service and encourage others to buy it or use it. Kids (and adults too) often find out about products and services when they talk to their friends. If a friend showed you a great new game, you might decide you want it too. Your parents may have found a house painter, landscaper, or car dealership by talking to their friends. Word of mouth is a powerful tool. Here are some ways to get people talking about your business.

Ask your satisfied customers to tell their friends. Let your customers know that you are looking for more business. Most people are happy to recommend a business that has provided them with good products and services.

Offer a referral discount. If a customer refers a friend and that friend buys your product or uses your service, then give your original customer a special discount or an additional service.

Tell your customers that you love seeing your business mentioned in social media. Facebook, Twitter, and Instagram can spread the word about your business.

Have an Online Presence

The Internet is an indispensable tool for business. The first thing many people do when they need a product or service is go online and search for what they want or need. They type keywords into an online search engine. The search engine then tells them what websites have the information they are looking for. If customers are looking for the product or service you offer, what words might they use? When you write the text for an ad or for a website, make sure to include the words a potential customer might use.

Are you included in a business directory? Are there lists of services like yours available online? Make sure your business has been added to those lists whenever possible.

Here are some important Internet terms to know as you set up your company's online presence.

A domain name is a unique name of a website. For example, if you and your friend have a lawn-mowing business, you might choose TwoPalsMowing.com as your domain name. You would register it and be the owner of that unique domain name.

Social networks are online communities. They can be a great way to get your business online without spending any money. It doesn't cost anything (and requires no special skills) to join a social network, like Facebook, Twitter, Instagram, or Pinterest. Talk to your parents about whether any of these social networks are right for you. If you are under 13, your parents will need to set up and run any social media accounts for you.

Maintaining a website online is web hosting. This usually costs money because websites take up space on a server (a computer set up to provide other computers with information). Many companies provide this service. Prices for web hosting can vary widely, so you should shop around. Many services offer a year of free web hosting before they start to charge you.

social networks
online communities where people connect and share common interests or contacts

Build a Website

Not every business needs a website, but a simple website can be a great marketing tool. And it's easier than ever to have your own website, even if you don't have any computer programming skills. The following sites provide you with basic templates and with a custom domain name. You just fill in information about your business. Most of these sites are free or inexpensive.

doodlekit.com

sitebuilder.com

websitebuilder.com

weebly.com

wordpress.com

wix.com

You can find other options by searching for "build simple websites" online.

When you write the text for your website, be clear. Think of all the questions your customers might ask you. And then be sure to include the answers to those questions on your site.

Stay Safe Online

Unfortunately, not everyone searching the Internet has good intentions, and it is important to be careful online. While you will need to give customers a way to get in touch with you, do not provide too much personal information. You should never give out your last name or your home address. Do not meet anybody who contacts you online in person (unless you are with a parent). And make sure that your parents always know whom you are in contact with online.

Conduct an Online Search

How would you find these products or services online? What keywords would you use? How are the search results different if you include the name of your town in your search? Are there adjectives or phrases that you can add to your search to find exactly what you want? Use a popular search engine like Google, Bing, or Yahoo! You can ask an adult to help.

TOPIC	WHAT KEYWORDS DO YOU USE?	YOUR TOP SEARCH ENGINE RESULTS	YOUR TOP SEARCH ENGINE RESULTS WHEN YOU INCLUDE THE NAME OF YOUR TOWN
Gardening			
Handmade jewelry			
Pet sitting			
Babysitting			
Dog walking			
Handmade soap			

Advertising Is Everywhere

When you log on to a computer or turn on the TV, you will see ads and commercials. There are ads at bus stops, on billboards, and in the pages of newspapers and magazines. Businesses usually pay to have their ads shown in these places. But there are plenty of free advertising opportunities as well. Your local supermarket, library, post office, and other town centers may have message boards. These can be great places to advertise your business!

Think creatively about where your target audience spends their time. If you have a dog-walking or dog-food delivery business, you might ask nearby veterinarians if you can post flyers in their offices. You might also paint a sign or sandwich board and display it at a local dog park. If you're starting an after-school crafts class for kids, you can approach local pediatricians or preschools about posting flyers on their message boards or including you in their newsletter.

WORDS FROM WARREN

Opening your mind can open the door to success.

Ad Basics

Wherever you decide to advertise, you'll have to create an ad. The basic components of an ad can be simple.

Include the name of the business and the company's logo.

Show an eye-catching drawing or a photograph that represents what the business does.

Provide a way to get in touch with the business: a website, email address, and/or phone number. Some locally placed flyers on bulletin boards include multiple copies of the business's contact information on strips along the bottom so people can tear off a strip and take it with them. It is important that you never share your personal email address, home address, or phone number without speaking to your parents first.

Other components may include a short description of the business, rates, or a tagline.

How Can Customers Reach You?

Together with your parents, decide what information you would like to provide to whom. You may feel comfortable including your email address or phone number to members of your church group or neighborhood association, but you may choose to keep your information private when posting information publicly. One way to deal with this issue is to have your parents create a separate email address for the business only, such as info@TomsTshirtDesigns.com or TomsTshirtDesigns@gmail.com. If you are doing business by mail, ask your parents to help you open a post office box. There will be a small monthly fee for the service—don't forget to add it to your expenses.

Design Your Own Ad

Flip through the newspaper and look at the advertisements. Look at the ads you see when you go online. Think about the ones that stand out the most to you. Using the basic rectangular ad layout below, design your own ad.

INCLUDE:

- The name of your business

- Your logo

- A tagline or description

- A great eye-catching image

- Contact information

Ad Placement

Once you have the basic layout you like, begin work on a final version. This can be hand drawn on paper or laid out on your computer. Once you have the basic components of your ad put together, you can use it to create ads in other shapes and sizes, such as flyers that can be posted on bulletin boards. If you are creating your ads by hand, make sure to scan them or take clear photos of them. That way, you can also have an emailable file of your ad to post on a website or send to someone to include in a newsletter.

When you have your final ad, figure out where you will reach the most people. Are there places in town where you can hang a flyer for free—at the grocery store, gym, book store, or skating rink? Can you post it on your town's Facebook page? If you're starting a snow-shoveling or car-washing business, can you walk around the neighborhood and put your flyer directly into people's mailboxes? Or tuck a flyer under the windshield wiper of cars near your home? If you want to start a business making family photo albums, can you hand out brochures in a local park—or post one on a local parents' association message board?

If this seems like work, you are right. Advertising is a business all its own. If you become really good at it, that could be your business!

What Is Publicity?

Publicity is when you or your business get mentioned in a newspaper, magazine, television or radio show, or on the Internet (in a blog, zine, or website). Publicity is free though businesses work very hard to get it. A publicist is a person whose job is to get publicity. The right piece of publicity can turn a tiny business into a big deal almost overnight.

Emily Matson and **Julianne Goldmark** were in the eighth grade when they started a hair accessories business, Emi-Jay. Emily's mother gave their accessories to a friend of hers who happened to be the stylist for actress Jennifer Aniston. After Aniston wore one of Emi-Jay's hair ties on the red carpet, an editor from the fashion magazine *Marie Claire* called, and Emi-Jay was put on the map.

Katelyn Lohr had been making her Freetoes (toeless socks) for friends and neighbors and selling them in local markets for several years. Her big break came when she appeared on a Canadian TV show called *Dragons' Den*. Suddenly, her business was transformed from one where her grandmother did all of the sewing and she hand-sold all of the socks into one where her product is manufactured in China and sold in hundreds of stores.

Madison Nicole Robinson created a line of flip-flops decorated with beachy designs. They are called FishFlops. A reporter for Yahoo! News noticed her tweets and became interested in her story. The reporter found out that although Madison was a social media whiz, she had gotten her FishFlops into Nordstrom (a major department store) in an old-fashioned way: She wrote the Nordstrom buyers a

publicity
the attention given to something (or someone) by the media. When a company appears in lots of newspapers, magazine, and blogs, it is getting lots of **publicity**.

letter. In 2013, the reporter posted her story, "How a 15-year-old entrepreneur got her product into Nordstrom," on the front page of the Yahoo! News website. The response was huge. Millions of people clicked on the article. Soon, Madison was receiving emails from retailers and distributors—and from customers who wanted to buy her product. Other reporters heard about Madison, and suddenly she was appearing on national TV news. The business quickly grew from sales in the hundreds to sales in the thousands. Sometimes a single article in the press can make all the difference to a business.

How Do I Get Publicity for My Business?

If you are very lucky, a reporter might find out about a great business run by a local kid and write a story about you. You can enter contests such as the Warren Buffett's Secret Millionaires Club "Grow Your Own Business Challenge" (smckids.com), where you might capture the attention of a reporter looking for a good story. But you can also reach out to writers at local newspapers and blogs. Contact producers of local TV news shows who might be interested in covering the story of an inspiring local young entrepreneur. Ask friends of your family if they know reporters or bloggers who might be interested in your story.

First you will need to prepare a press release. A press release is a short write-up about your business featuring some newsworthy information. A kid starting a business might be newsworthy to a local newspaper. Or the fact that you are using an old family recipe might appeal to certain journalists. Send over your press release and then follow up with a telephone call or an email. A writer may then interview you or incorporate information from your press release into a story.

It is important to note that sending a reporter a press release does not guarantee that he or she will write about you. Many, many people and companies send out press releases every day. It can be difficult to get a reporter's attention. To capture a journalist's attention, you want to make sure your press release is timely and your story is newsworthy. Here are a few newsworthy reasons to issue a press release.

→ You are launching a new product.

→ Your product is unusual or different.

→ You have just landed a big deal to sell your products to a major retailer.

→ You've just won an award or a contest.

→ You've done something noteworthy in your community (such as volunteered or made a donation to local group or family).

→ You offer a product or service that relates to an upcoming holiday or event.

→ You are the youngest entrepreneur to be recognized or to participate in an event in your community.

→ Your product or service ties in with another item in the news. (For example, if a scientist releases a study that says eating local honey or using goats' milk soap has incredible health benefits, you can reach out to reporters to let them know you are available to talk about your locally produced honey or goats' milk soap.)

How to Write a Press Release

A press release has a special format that lets reporters find the information they want quickly. Here are the components of a press release.

FOR IMMEDIATE RELEASE—This appears at the top left of the page in upper case letters. It tells reporters that they can let the world know about your news right away.

Headline—A good headline will grab the reporter's attention. The headline is one short, punchy sentence highlighting the most newsworthy, exciting part of your story.

City, state, date—Put these details in right before the body of your story.

Body—This tells your story. It is usually a few paragraphs long and may include a quote from the owner of the company (you).

Company information—The press release should contain a brief description of your company and include your company's website or address.

Contact information—Provide your name, email, and telephone number here. The reporter may want to get in touch with you for more details.

Your entire press release should fit on one sheet of paper.

Tell a Great Story

Reporters are just like everyone else. They love charming, funny stories. If there is a cool story about how you came up with the idea for your company, include it in your release. For example, perhaps you started baking gluten-free cookies because you found out you were allergic to gluten but couldn't give up sweets. A cute story like that might spark the writer's interest.

Sample Press Release

10-YEAR-OLD LAUNCHES LINE OF SHARK CRAFTS JUST
IN TIME FOR SHARK WEEK

FABULOUSTOWN, PA (May 20, 2016) Ten-year-old Erika Jones is launching her line of handmade shark crafts, FuzzyFins, on July 1, 2016—just in time for Shark Week. The line includes squeezable fabric crafts that are soft, portable, and fun.

When Erika was 8 years old, a live shark washed up on the shore while she was on vacation with her family. She saw a group of people help the shark by getting it back out into the open water. That's when she became hooked on sharks. She read lots of books about them and began sewing shark pouches and stuffed animals. "I created FuzzyFins because I love sharks and I love to sew," said Erika.

The first FuzzyFins craft line includes:

Great White Wallets—These felt pouches are great for gobbling up loose change.

Hammerhead Pillows—Made from colorful fabric scraps, these fun pillows are in the shape of hammerhead sharks.

Whale Shark Snugglies—Whale sharks are the biggest sharks in the ocean, and Whale Shark Snugglies are FuzzyFins' biggest craft. These polka-dotted plush toys are awesome for cuddling.

Blue Shark Buddies—Like actual blue sharks, Blue Shark Buddies are darker on top than they are on their bellies. Blue Shark Buddies love to go on adventures!

Erika hopes to add new products, such as headbands and bracelets, to the line by the fall so they will be available for the holidays.

ABOUT FUZZYFINS

Erika created FuzzyFins to celebrate her favorite animal, the shark. "So many people think sharks are ferocious and that they like to bite people," says Erika, "but they are wrong. Sharks are incredible ocean animals, and we should all work to protect their habitat." Erika is committed to helping endangered sharks and preventing people from harming sharks. She donates 20% of the proceeds from the sale of FuzzyFins crafts to Shark Savers, a nonprofit organization dedicated to saving sharks.

For more information about Erika Jones and FuzzyFins or to see photos of Erika and the FuzzyFins crafts, visit FuzzyFins.com.

CONTACT: Erika Jones, FuzzyFins@gmail.com, (555) 670-2391

Try It Out

Try writing a press release for your business so you can get your story out!

FOR IMMEDIATE RELEASE

_____

[Headline]

_____ , _____ (_____)

[City, State (Date)]

_____

_____

_____

_____

_____

_____

_____

_____

_____

_____

_____

_____

_____

Contact: _____

Promotions, Incentives, Premiums, and Sales

In addition to benefiting from word of mouth, gaining a web presence, placing advertisements, and getting publicity, you can also run marketing campaigns that include promotions, incentives, premiums, and sales.

Plan a promotion.
Promotions are short-term special offers designed to get customers' attention. Examples of promotions include offering two-for-one lemonades on the first day of summer or holding a raffle that provides a lucky customer with a free service. If you do hold a raffle or contest, it's a great idea to collect people's email addresses as they enter the contest. This way, you can build an email list to use the next time you want to alert people about a new product or special offer.

Offer incentives.
Incentives are offers that make people want to do more business with you. You might offer 10% off a service if a customer tells a neighbor about your great service. Or you could give a free dog bath with every tenth walk. If you are selling items online, you could offer free shipping to anyone who spends a certain amount of money. Try different incentives and see which ones work best with your customers.

Put items on sale.
You see sales all the time—at the mall, at the supermarket, and online. Sales, or offering discounts off of the regular price, are a proven way to get customers to do more business. You can try running a sale on your products or services. "This week only—two dog walks for the price of one" and "Buy two friendship bracelets and get the third for free" are two examples of sales.

Experiment with different approaches to publicity, promotion, and advertising, and see what delivers the best results. Then keep it up!

WORDS FROM WARREN

Always promote yourself. Successful businesses successfully promote and advertise themselves.

CHAPTER 8.

WHAT'S YOUR BUSINESS PLAN?

Now that you've learned a lot about
starting and promoting a business,
it's time to get out a pencil and get
to work. Planning ahead can help
you identify problems—and avoid
them—before they even arise. These
worksheets will help you think
through your business before you
get started.

What Is a Business Plan?

A business plan is a written description of your business and its goals. Successful businesses always begin with a solid plan. Writing a business plan is a great way to wrap your head around the business you are building. It helps you put your vision into words, and it will help you work toward your goals. Plus, having a written business plan will surely impress your parents or mentors or anyone you may approach for a loan, investment, or mentorship.

WORDS FROM WARREN

Fail to plan, plan to fail.

A business plan should include:

→ Information about your business (what it does)

→ Information about who your business serves (your customers and your marketplace)

→ Information about your competition (and what you do that is different or better than your competition)

→ Your financial plan (start-up costs, budget, and profit and loss statement) and your operational plan (how you are going to make it happen)

What Your Business Does

Every business plan begins with a description of the business. Here's your chance to explain why your idea is a good one. The words should be simple and as clear as possible.

Imagine a company that sells homemade granola in the park on Saturdays and Sundays during community sports practices and games. How would you describe this business? It might go something like this:

> GARY'S GREATEST GRANOLA COMPANY—ABOUT THE COMPANY
> Gary's Greatest Granola Company brings local athletes, their parents, and their fans the best-tasting and healthiest granola available in Howard County. We make our delicious granola from all-natural ingredients and sell it from our Gary's Greatest Granola wagon on weekends during practices and games.

Now You Try It

Write a short description of your company to include in your business plan.

_____

_____

_____

_____

_____

_____

_____

_____

_____

WORDS FROM WARREN

Keep it simple. Don't get involved in a business you don't understand.

Who Your Business Serves

Who are your customers? What need is your product or service fulfilling? What does the market for your service look like? Be as specific as you can be about who will buy your product or use your service.

Nick Lavery always loved making videos. He looked around at his classmates and thought about his own interests and came up with a great idea for a business. He would film games and create highlight reels for players on his school's sports teams. It was clear who his customers were: basketball players, football players, and other athletes. He knew these athletes would want to have a record of their accomplishments to show friends, family members, and coaches. Plus, Nick sets his videos to music, so they are lots of fun to watch. And his market could easily grow to other schools and other athletes or performers in the area.

GARY'S GREATEST GRANOLA COMPANY—MARKETPLACE
Gary's Greatest Granola Company sells granola snacks in Centennial Park on Saturdays and Sundays, when it is filled with kids and families who come for sports practices and games. Playing sports all day, these kids work up an appetite. They're always ready for a snack when they walk off the field. Customers know they can rely on Gary's Greatest Granola Company to be in the same place at the same times. They know that we make great breakfasts and healthy midday snacks. Our treats are priced right too, making them affordable for the families and kids who spend their time in the park.

Now You Try It
Describe your customers and why they need your product or service.

Your Competition

Does your company have any competition? If so, what will you do differently than other companies? How does your product stand out? Why do you believe there is room for another player in that market?

GARY'S GREATEST GRANOLA COMPANY—COMPETITION
There are some other food vendors in the park on the weekend. An ice cream truck sells ice cream and sweet drinks, but it moves around so the kids and families by the practice fields cannot always count on it to be there when they are hungry. There is also a hot dog vendor. Unlike the ice cream truck and the hot dog vendor, I sell healthy food made with all-natural ingredients. Gary's Greatest Granola is the only company in the park that offers a healthy breakfast and a healthy snack. Many of the parents in the park want their kids to eat natural foods that aren't so high in calories and fat. And many of the people in the park are there running, cycling, or practicing with their sports teams. There's a bustling market of health-conscious consumers ready to try my food.

Now You Try It

Write a brief description of the other companies or products that are like yours. Then explain how your product or service is different or better.

_____

_____

_____

_____

_____

_____

_____

_____

_____

_____

_____

_____

_____

_____

_____

_____

Your Budget

You'll need to include a **budget** in your business plan. Everyone should develop a monthly budget to organize their income and expenses. Having a budget helps you keep track of your money and spend it more wisely. With a budget, you'll be sure that you have enough money to buy the things you need. Another big reason why a budget is so important is that it serves as a plan to save money.

How to Set Up a Business Budget

To make a budget for your business, write down all of your income—the money you have coming in from jobs you've completed or items sold. Then write down all of your expenses—all those things you spend money on such as doggie shampoo and combs for your pet-grooming business.

Add up your income. Add up your expenses. Subtract total expenses from total income. This is your **bottom line**.

> **Total Income — Total Expenses = Bottom Line**

Is it a positive number? Then, congratulations! You are **in the black**. In other words, you are making money! Is the number negative? This means you are spending more than you are making and your business is **in the red**. If your total income and your total expenses are the same, then your bottom line will be zero. You are not making money or losing money. You have a balanced budget.

It's okay to operate "at a loss" sometimes. That means you are in the red, or losing money, for a period of time. You may be investing in expensive equipment (like a lawn mower, food processor, computer hard drive, or new sewing machine), or it

budget
a plan that shows how much money you will earn and what expenses you expect to have over a certain period of time

bottom line
the last line on a budget. If it is a positive number, your company has a profit. If it is negative, the company has a loss.

in the black
when you are bringing in more money as income than you are spending on expenses. Positive numbers are shown in black ink on budgets. A company that makes money is **in the black**.

in the red
when you are spending more money on expenses than you are bringing in as income. Negative numbers are often shown in red ink on company budgets. A company that is losing money is **in the red**.

The most important thing to do if you find yourself in a hole is to stop digging.

may simply be an off-month for you. Most companies have months that are busy and months that are slow. But if you are in the red month after month, you will have to reevaluate your business.

Sample Budget

This is a sample budget for Lori's Well-Read Books, a used bookstore that Lori operates through an online store. This is what Lori's business budget looks like for the month of August.

AUGUST BUDGET FOR LORI'S WELL-READ BOOKS			
Income	**Amount**	**Expenses**	**Cost**
20 books sold for an average of $4 each	$80	20 used books purchased at a library sale	$30
		Postage	$10
		Packing materials	$5
		Transaction/hosting fees for website	$5
TOTAL INCOME	$80	TOTAL EXPENSES	$50

PROFIT AND LOSS STATEMENT FOR AUGUST	
Total income	$80
minus	
Total expenses	$50
Profit (or loss, if this is a negative number)	$30

Lori made a profit of $30!

Evaluate Your Business

To get an even better idea of how Lori's business is doing, let's look at her profit per unit and her hourly wage. To find out Lori's profit per unit, take her total profit and divide it by the number of units she sold.

Total Profit		Number of Units Sold		Profit per Unit
$30	÷	20	=	$1.50

Lori made an average of $1.50 on every book she sold.

How much did Lori make per hour of work? Lori spent 10 hours during the month running her business—buying books, selling them online, and shipping them to customers. She made $30 in profit. To find out how much Lori earned per hour, Lori would have to divide her total monthly profit by the number of hours that she spent working.

WORDS FROM WARREN

Someone is sitting in the shade today because someone planted a tree a long time ago.

Total Monthly Profit		Number of Hours Spent Working		Income per Hour (or Hourly Wage)
$30	÷	10	=	$3

Lori made $3 for every hour she worked.

Knowing numbers such as profit per unit and income per hour can help Lori decide if she wants to continue her business. If she can earn $10 an hour babysitting, she may decide her bookselling business is not worth her time. Or she may decide that she likes her business so much that she doesn't mind earning less money doing it.

Now You Try It

Create a budget for your business. If your business is up and running, use real numbers. If your business is still just an idea in your head, you can make a good guess (this is called a **projected** budget).

projected
planned or estimated for sometime in the future

Business Name

Income	Amount	Expenses	Cost
	$		$
	$		$
	$		$
	$		$
	$		$
	$		$
	$		$
Total Income	$	**Total Expenses**	$

Profit and Loss Statement for _____
[Month]

Total Income minus **Total Expenses**	$_____ $_____
Profit (or loss, if this is a negative number)	$_____

Make a profit and loss statement (P&L) every month to see how your business is doing. And take a few minutes to calculate your hourly wage to see how much money you are making for each hour you work on your business.

CHAPTER 9.

SAVING, INVESTING, AND SPENDING

As a businessperson, you will have to decide how much of your earnings you will save, how much you will invest back into your business, and how much you will spend. One of the most important lessons in business is the importance of saving. It's a great habit to learn early in life.

Savings Can Save You

If you are just beginning to think about starting your own business, a savings account can help you put away money for the start-up costs. If you have a business already, putting money in a savings account will be a big help if some of your equipment breaks. Savings can also come in handy if you get an unusually large order and need to buy lots of supplies. It is always a good idea to have extra money saved up in case of an emergency.

Saving the money you make in your business can help you expand when the time is right. (For more on growing your business, see Chapter 10.) You can also use the money you save for your future—to help pay for college or to use as spending money while you are in college, to buy a car, or even to put a down payment on a house.

WORDS FROM WARREN

The biggest mistake is not learning the habits of saving properly early. Because saving is a habit.

interest
payment given to a lender in exchange for letting a bank or a person borrow money for a period of time

Madison Nicole Robinson, founder of the successful flip-flop brand FishFlops, doesn't touch the profits from her business. Because of her dedication to saving, she has already put away enough money for college. When she wants to buy something, she uses money saved from birthdays or holidays.

Opening a Savings Account

Banks are places that hold other people's money for them. When you put money into a savings account at the bank, the money cannot be lost or stolen. Many banks will let kids open a savings account for free with any amount of money. Sometimes banks require a minimum deposit. That means you have to have a certain amount of money to put into the account and to keep there. You may want to call ahead or look online to see if your local bank or your parents' bank has a minimum deposit.

When you leave your money with the bank, they will often pay you a very small amount for letting them keep your money. This is called interest. Similarly, when you borrow money from the bank, you will need to pay back the amount you borrowed, plus some extra (in interest) for keeping the bank's money over a certain period of time.

Investing in Your Business

Putting some of your earnings back into your business makes sense if you want your business to grow. If you offer a product, such as a snack or a cup of lemonade, you may want to invest money in a wagon to take your business on the road. You may even have your sights set on a food truck at some point in the future. If you offer a service such as walking dogs or watering plants, you may want to put some money into advertising to get more customers. If you use a computer for designing websites, developing apps, or creating sports highlights reels, you may need to pay for new software or upgrades. If you're a DJ, you may want to download more music or invest in new equipment.

Sometimes it makes the most sense to invest your earnings in your next business. For example, **Farrhad Acidwalla** invested some of the earnings from the sale of his first business into his next business. Several years after he sold his company (an online community dedicated to airplanes and aviation), he put $400 of his earnings into Rockstah Media, which has grown into a hugely successful international communications company.

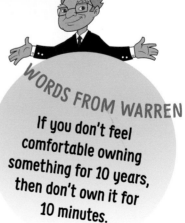

WORDS FROM WARREN

If you don't feel comfortable owning something for 10 years, then don't own it for 10 minutes.

Spending—Finding the Right Balance

Most people who work hard like to spend at least some of their money on things that make their lives better, more interesting, and more fun. It can be a big reason why kids (and grown-ups too) start businesses. Mark Cuban sold trash bags because he wanted to buy a pair of sneakers. He earned that money and went on to earn much, much more. Lizzie Marie Likness started her baking business because she wanted to take horseback-riding lessons. She earned enough for her lessons and more.

Think of the things you would like to do with the money you earn—buy a new game, get a new sweater, attend a performance or sporting event, or buy gifts for your friends and family. Now think about the long-term goals you may have for your earnings, such as paying for your gymnastics lessons or soccer camp, buying a bicycle or a car, saving for college, or putting money away for a trip to South America after college.

Spending Wishlist

"Look, a cool shirt!" "The new superhero movie just hit theaters!" "Sure, I'll take a large popcorn with that!" "Oooh, I want those new sneakers." If you buy all of the things you see that you like, you will quickly find that all of your money is gone. It is a good idea to remind yourself how much things cost by making a list of what you'd like to do with your money. Write down the costs of the things you would like to buy soon and in the near future, and the things you would like to save for.

THINGS I'D LIKE TO BUY SOON	THINGS I'D LIKE TO BUY IN THE NEAR FUTURE	THINGS I'D LIKE TO SAVE FOR	COST
New skateboard			$50 total
Hockey jersey			$65 total
	Tickets to see a Broadway show with my family		$300 total
	A mountain bike		$500 total
		Spending money for college	$50/month
		Savings in case of an emergency	$50/month

When you've made a list of all the things you'd like to save money for and spend money on, then look at the amount of money you are making every month and set some financial goals. A good habit to get into is to make sure you are saving some amount each month—and that you put your savings ahead of your spending.

earmark

say that something is set aside for a specific purpose

Make a Personal Budget

Just like you made a budget for your business, you can make a budget for yourself. Write down all of your personal income and expenses, and make some decisions about what you'd most like to do with your money.

If you are making $200 a month, perhaps you will decide to spend $50 of that money each month (on movie tickets, pizza with friends, and other small stuff). You could set $50 aside each month for one of your big-ticket items (like those Broadway show tickets or a bike) and save $100 each month. Of that $100 per month savings, you may **earmark** $50 for the business and $50 for your own long-term savings goals.

It can be tough to balance your desire to buy things with your commitment to saving and investing, but if you make a plan and stick to it, it is easier to reach your goals. Spending money wisely is part of being a good businessperson.

CHAPTER 10

GROWING YOUR BUSINESS

Once you get the hang of something—babysitting, editing videos, baking muffins, flower arranging—it may be time to grow your business. You might be ready for more customers, additional products, maybe even hiring an employee or opening a second location.

Grow Your Profits

So your business is up and running. And you are making some money, but you think you might be able to do better. It's important to evaluate your business. What can you do to increase your profits?

Lower your costs. Find ways to save money on supplies, equipment, labor, advertising—anything that costs your business money. But be careful here. If you are known for your organic lemonade with all-natural ingredients and you decide to start using a powdered lemonade mix instead to save money, you might increase your profits for the short-term. But you would hurt your brand over the longer term. You would probably lose customers. However, there are ways to save money that would not hurt the quality of your product. Buying supplies or ingredients in bulk or buying items on sale are all smart ways to lower costs and increase profits.

Charge more. Your business will be more profitable if you can charge more for your goods or services. Here, too, a business owner has to be careful. Make sure you understand your customers. If you go from charging $10 a day to walk a dog to $50 a day with no explanation or without adding additional services, it is likely that your customers would stop using you. It is also important to look at the supply of and demand for your product. If you charge $5 for a cupcake when there are other nearby cupcake stands selling their sweets for $2 apiece, it is likely that your sales would suffer. But not all price increases are a bad idea. It's possible that you are not charging enough money. Take a look at the cupcake market in your town for clues. If your 25-cent cupcakes are flying off the shelves, they may still sell quickly at 50 cents or even $1 apiece.

Do more business with your customers. You can grow your business—a lot—if you focus on doing more business with the customers you already have. Ask your customers for feedback. Ask them what you could be doing better and then follow through on their suggestions. People like to know their opinion matters. Figure out what you're doing right, and do more of it. Try out new products on your loyal customers. If they love your healthy muffins, see if they might like fresh brewed iced tea, biscuits, or bread. By trying out your business expansion ideas on the clients you already know, you may learn from their reactions and decide if your new product ideas are worth pursuing.

Find more customers. You can usually make more money by doing more—selling more flowers, shoveling more driveways, or tutoring more kids. Use referrals, sales, freebies, and other incentives to attract new customers. Another way to do more business is to expand your opportunity to sell. You may be able to sell more T-shirts in the same amount of time if you move to a busier location or if you have a sale. But everyone is limited by the amount of time they have. You cannot be in two places at once. You'll have to figure out how much it is possible for you to do or make. Maybe it is time to hire a helper. But will the extra money earned be enough to pay for your new employee's time? Or would your new employee be willing to work for a percentage of the profits he or she brings in? Make projections, do the math ahead of time, and make an informed decision about hiring.

feedback
information and opinions about how to make something better

Share What You Know
The most successful business owners share information with others. By being open and communicating, you will exchange information that might help you solve a problem or come up with more good ideas. And you will learn even more about your business.

WORDS FROM WARREN

Whether we're talking about socks or stocks, I like buying quality merchandise when it is marked down.

Be more efficient. Sometimes you can decrease the amount of time it takes you to prepare your products if you work more efficiently. Perhaps you usually decorate the boxes that your cookies are sold in as you get orders. It might be more efficient to work on many boxes at once or to decorate the boxes while each batch of cookies is in the oven instead. Maybe you spend a lot of time each week biking back and forth from the art-supply store. It might be more efficient if you pick up more supplies less often. Then you can spend those freed-up hours making and selling more product.

Grow to Meet Customer Needs

Sometimes businesses grow because smart owners are in tune with what their customers want and need.

Ingvar Kamprad grew up in a small farming community in Sweden, far from stores. When he was only 5 years old, Ingvar noticed that his neighbors always needed matches. Ingvar bought matches in bulk at wholesale prices and then went from house to house, selling them. Ingvar had found such a low price on the matches in bulk that he was able to give his customers a good price and still make a profit. By 7, he was using his bike to expand his territory. From matches, he moved to selling fish, Christmas tree decorations, seeds, pens, and pencils. Ingvar kept figuring out what the people in his remote community needed. And then he bought lots of those items cheaply and sold them for a profit. His neighbors were happy to pay for the convenience of buying the things they needed without having to travel. Ingvar's clever door-to-door business eventually grew into IKEA, the world's largest furniture company.

Sarkis Johnson started his skateboard company, Liquid Chicken, when he was just 12 years old. He sold skateboard decks, T-shirts, and grip tape. Often when a customer bought a skateboard deck from Liquid Chicken, he or she would ask for the rest of the parts that make up a skateboard, such as the wheels and the trucks (the metal parts that attach the wheels to the deck), and other skateboard accessories. As Sarkis grows his business, he plans to add these items to his list.

How can you figure out what your customers need? How can you provide it to them? Answering those questions will help you to grow your business to meet the needs of your customers.

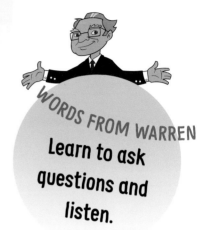

WORDS FROM WARREN
Learn to ask questions and listen.

Grow to Learn New Skills

As a business owner, you should always be learning. Learning new things and using your new skills and knowledge to grow your business are some of the best parts of owning a business. Consider these business ideas. What new skills can you learn to grow these businesses? We've given you some examples. Add some of your own ideas.

BUSINESS	SKILLS NEEDED	SKILLS TO LEARN AND GROW
Selling dog food and dog treats	Reliability, ability to read and follow a recipe, attention to detail, cleanliness	Learn more about pet health and develop more recipes—to help with allergies in dogs or to make dog chews that are good for dog's teeth and breath. Make cat food as well.
Making wallets out of colored duct tape	Craftiness, creativity, attention to detail	Learn to make and sell more complex crafts with metal or Velcro clasps and closures.

BUSINESS	SKILLS NEEDED	SKILLS TO LEARN AND GROW
Writing tutor	Good with kids, knowledge of writing styles and techniques	Learn about website design and maintenance to start an online literary magazine. Or learn about planning and hosting events and then host a reading series or book club.
Lemonade stand	Ability to read a recipe and measure	Experiment with different flavor combinations, then design and print recipe booklets with your favorite recipes.
Homemade friendship bracelets	Patience, attention to detail, creativity	Learn more detailed designs. Create new products such as necklaces, belts, key rings, or headbands using the design, weaving, and knotting skills you've learned.

Smart Borrowing to Boost Your Business

Sometimes it is necessary to borrow money to expand a business. It's important to be realistic and cautious when borrowing money or taking out bank loans. Make sure you know all about your business's profits and expenses, and study your market before taking on any debt.

Emil Motycka's first landscaping job was mowing his aunt and uncle's lawn when he was 8 years old. He didn't even have a trimmer, so he used scissors to finish the job. As he got more jobs, he got better and faster and started to learn about what kind of equipment would help his business. One day, when Emil was 13, he watched a competitor finish a job in a quarter of the time it would have taken him. The other business had a commercial lawn mower. By watching his competitor at work, Emil learned how he could do his job better. He determined that, with the right equipment, he could mow even more lawns. He researched the costs of the equipment and did some math to determine how the new equipment could result in more profits.

Emil asked his parents to cosign an $8,000 loan so he could buy a commercial-grade lawn mower. It was a four-year loan. Emil paid it off in just two years. Emil was able to get his lawn mower, expand his business, and build good credit. In the future, if Emil needs to borrow money to buy a car or a home or to invest in a business, a bank can look at his credit history and see that he has paid off a loan—and paid it off early.

Change It Up!

Your customers' needs and tastes could change. And your own interests may change. Then it might be time to change your business too. Your snow cone customers from the summer probably won't want a frozen treat when there's frost on the windows. But they might be thrilled if you showed up with hot chocolate for sale at the local sledding hill. If you are an in-demand lawn mower in the summer, the same customers may want to hire you to shovel their driveways in the winter.

As seasons and needs change, you will change too! Maybe your schedule is suddenly busy with sports practice and you can't walk dogs after

cosign
to sign along with someone else. When a parent **cosigns** a loan, he or she is promising to pay back the loan if the child cannot.

WORDS FROM WARREN

It is impossible to unsign a contract, so do all your thinking before you sign.

school anymore. Think about offering weekend dog grooming instead. Or maybe you once really enjoyed making bracelets to sell but are now interested in weaving baskets or painting pottery. You can move your business in any direction you like. That is one of the most interesting and fun parts of owning your own business.

Let your business grow along with you. **Tavi Gevinson** started her fashion blog, *Style Rookie*, when she was 11. When she felt that she and her readers had outgrown that blog, she started Rookie (rookiemag.com), a website for teens. She even published three print collections of her magazine. She's been so successful at finding her niche that she helped to launch a clothing line, and she's been interviewed countless times for her style expertise. She has also appeared in movies and on Broadway.

You can even move on to a new business.

Cameron Johnson started out designing cards. Then he decided to sell Beanie Babies. Next, he created an email service and sold advertising space. After that, he created an online advertising company. Cameron created a few successful businesses before he was even out of high school. Now he talks to kids and adults about starting businesses.

CHAPTER 11

GIVING BACK

Good business isn't just about making money. It's about contributing to the world and making it a better place. If you plant gardens, tutor younger children, or make products that people enjoy, you are already doing something good. But you can do more. Think about the causes that are important to you. How can you or your business help? And remember— donating your time can be just as valuable as donating money.

How Can You Contribute?

Many business owners support causes that are close to their hearts. What are the causes you care the most about? Can you make those causes part of your business?

Mikaila Ulmer, the founder of BeeSweet Lemonade, was only 4 years old when she was stung by a bee— twice. Mikaila didn't like being stung, but she did become interested in bees. She found out that bees play an important part in our ecosystem. As they fly around, they pick up pollen from flowers. They carry this pollen to other flowers, which makes it possible for the plants to produce seeds. In this way, bees help the crops that give us food. And bees have been dying off in big numbers. Mikaila thought about how much the bees help us, and she wanted to help them in return.

Mikaila turned to her great-grandmother's recipe for flaxseed lemonade. She sweetened it with local Texas honey and created BeeSweet Lemonade. Mikaila gives a portion of her profits to organizations that help bees. And she volunteers her time teaching people about how they can help save the honeybee.

Asya Gonzalez started Stinky Feet Gurlz in 2011, when she was 14 years old. But she had more than just business on the brain. Her goal was to help victims of child sex trafficking. Asya sells T-shirts that feature a character named Weezie, along with other 1940s-inspired designs, on her website. She donates a portion of every sale to help prevent the trafficking of girls and women. She has also created a foundation to increase awareness of the problem of trafficking.

Aanikh Kler says kids don't have to wait until they become adults to change the world. And he's a great example of a kid making a difference. On a trip to Cambodia when he was 13 years old, he saw young children working all day under the hot sun to help buy food for their families. He began thinking about how some children do not have the same opportunities as he does. Later, something happened at school that gave him a great idea—both for business and for helping others. A friend's cell phone went off during class, and the teacher took it away. Aanikh did some research and discovered something interesting about humans' ears: as people age, their hearing changes. There are frequencies of sound that most people under the age of 21 can hear that most people over 21 cannot. He set out to—and succeeded in—making a cell phone ringtone that adults can't hear.

Aanikh calls his ringtone app UndrTheRadr. From the very beginning, he wanted to help children who were also "under the radar." For every 99-cent download of his ringtone, he donates 20 cents to Free The Children. This incredible organization (which was also founded by a teen!) is dedicated to children helping other children worldwide. It aims to keep children safe and out of poverty through education. Aanikh was one of the youngest app developers to have the #2 most downloaded paid app in the iTunes App Store. And the proceeds from his app have helped countless children around the world.

WORDS FROM WARREN

If you're in the luckiest 1% of humanity, you owe it to the rest of humanity to think about the other 99%.

112

philanthropy
giving money and time to make life better for other people

Lutece Kramer-Guillemot and **Tess Olmi**, who design and sell handmade, one-of-a-kind beads through their company, Marbelous, give a portion of every sale to their favorite charities, Heeling Autism and Every Mother Counts. They also found a clever way to tie their branding to their commitment to **philanthropy**. Their mission is "to make the world a more marbelous place."

Emily Matson and **Julianne Goldmark**, the young founders of Emi-Jay hair accessories, donate 20% of their profits to their favorite charities, including Children's Hospital Los Angeles.

All of these entrepreneurs embraced the idea of giving back early on and have incorporated it into their business models.

Packaging with a Purpose

Remember Hart Main, the founder of ManCans? He uses recycled soup cans as packaging for his candles, and he found a way to get the supplies he needs while helping people. Hart's company buys soup and donates it to soup kitchens. After the soup kitchens serve the soup, they return the empty cans to Hart to use in his business.

Doing Well By Doing Good

Being a good citizen and a good neighbor is almost always good for business. Madison Nicole Robinson, creator of FishFlops, wanted her fun designs to be enjoyed by kids who couldn't afford to buy them. So she's given her shoes away all over the world.

When she donated FishFlops to military children, she received a major order from the Army's Post Exchange stores. A few years ago, she convinced celebrities at the 2011 Teen Choice Awards to sign 300 pairs of FishFlops. Then she gave the super-special shoes to patients at the Texas Children's Hospital to brighten their days. Bloggers wrote about this gift, and more people heard about FishFlops. The press also loved talking about it when Madison donated 10,000 pairs of FishFlops to a community shoe drive and when she supported the Texas Parks & Wildlife's K-12 State-Fish Art Contest. Her good deeds have not gone unnoticed, and her business has done well as a result of the positive publicity.

Match Your Passion to a Cause

Like Aanikh did, perhaps you can match a great business idea to a cause that means a lot to you. Think of a cause you care about. Can you start a business that could help that cause? Is there a cause that relates to the work you're already doing? Here are some ideas.

Do you sell cold drinks in your local park during softball and soccer games? Think about donating a portion of your profits to a local team. You may even be able to **sponsor** a team. Team sponsorships (when a business pays a fee to help cover the costs of the league, and their name goes on players' shirts) can be good publicity as well.

sponsor
to give money or time to help another person, team, or cause

Do you sell used books? Consider supporting a cause that gets more people to read. Your local library or a literacy organization would love to hear from you!

Do you sell healthy snacks? You could run a canned food drive for a local soup kitchen or lend a helping hand.

Do you run a website about endangered species? Donate some of your profits to wildlife conservation groups or animal sanctuaries—or offer them free advertising on your site.

Are you a dog walker or cat sitter? Volunteer your time at an animal shelter.

Do you run a lawn-mowing business? Offer your services, for free, to a nearby nonprofit.

WORDS FROM WARREN

Many people, including—I'm proud to say—my three children, give extensively of their own time and talents to help others. Gifts of this kind often prove far more valuable than money.

Volunteer to Learn Something New

Volunteering can be a great way to give back, meet new customers, and learn new skills.

Are you a dog walker? Would you like to expand into obedience training or pet grooming? The local animal shelter may be looking for extra hands, and the employees there may be able to teach you what you want to learn.

Do you mow lawns but aspire to offer your customers landscape design? The local gardening club may be excited to talk with you.

Are you an up-and-coming blogger? Volunteer to guest blog for a local charity. You'll learn more about blogging—and you'll get your name and your website out there.

Is your business related to your favorite sport? Did you know that many athletes get injured while playing? Contact a sports rehab facility and see if they need volunteers. You might learn about physical therapy and injury prevention while you're there.

Are you a writer, a radio host, or a DJ? Volunteer your time at a senior living facility. Host storytelling groups, talk to the elderly who live there, or play music for a social hour. You'll probably get some great ideas for stories, or learn about some music you've never listened to before.

Products with Purpose

Moziah Bridges, the creator of Mo's Bows, decided he would make one product that would be 100% for charity. He created the Go Mo Summer Camp Bow Tie specifically to help kids go to summer camp. "I feel like it's good to help the community, and that's what I'm doing," Moziah says.

Gabrielle Jordan also made a specific product to benefit a cause. She designed a pink beaded bracelet as part of her Jewelz of Jordan line to raise money for young women with breast cancer.

Is Setting Up a Nonprofit Right for You?

While many businesspeople make sure to denote their time or money to the causes they support, some businesses are formed specifically to work for a cause or a community. These organizations are called nonprofits. Nonprofits generally try to keep their operating costs low so the income they generate is used for their mission (rather than giving the income to the owner or owners as profit).

Some nonprofits have been started by kids just like you.

Help other kids. Like a lot of young people, **Alexandra "Alex" Scott** wanted to open a lemonade stand. She was just 4 years old. But that's not what makes Alex's business unique. Alex opened up her lemonade stand because she had cancer and she wanted to raise money so that more doctors could help more kids just like her.

Her first lemonade stand, in 2000, raised $2,000. It wasn't long before Alex's idea became the nonprofit, Alex's Lemonade Stand Foundation. Four years later, at the age of 8, Alex passed away. By then, she had raised more than $1 million for cancer research. She made a big impact on the world through her amazing spirit and her contribution.

Today, Alex's Lemonade Stand Foundation sponsors a national fundraising weekend every June called Alex's Lemonade Days. Thousands of volunteers raise money for cancer research at more than 20,000 Alex's Lemonade Stands around the country.

Make a big difference by doing something small. In 2008, third-grader **Katie Stagliano** grew an enormous 40-pound cabbage. Knowing it was a very special vegetable, she donated the giant cabbage to a soup kitchen in her hometown of Summerville, South Carolina. It helped to feed more than 275 people! Katie couldn't believe how something she enjoyed doing—gardening—could help so many people. So Katie planted more vegetables and donated more harvests. Today, Katie's nonprofit, Katie's Krops, gives thousands of pounds of vegetables from numerous gardens to organizations that help people in need.

Save Earth and its animals. Dakota Palacio first became interested in conservation when she found out that a special kind of bear (called the spirit bear) was at risk because of the actions of logging companies in Canada. Dakota felt that kids could make a difference when it came to conservation. She opened her own nonprofit, Beholdance, when she was just 13 years old. Beholdance is a conservation and community service organization designed to get other kids involved with volunteering and helping the environment and endangered species.

How Will You Make a Difference?

What causes are important to you? How can you help? How can your business help?

There are so many ways to change the world for the better, especially if you are an entrepreneur. You can create a product or service that helps people or the environment. You can give away some of the things you create. You can use your skills to help people and animals. You can donate some of the money you make. You can even set up your own nonprofit to help a cause you believe in. However you decide to better the world, make it part of your business plan.

WORDS FROM WARREN

There are an unlimited number of good things to be done in the world.

CHAPTER 12.

SECRETS OF SUCCESSFUL ENTREPRENEURS

People who start their own businesses—entrepreneurs—are different from other people but similar to each other in a few key ways. They have what is sometimes called an "entrepreneurial spirit." Among other qualities, they're usually brave (it can be scary and risky to start your own business). They're persistent. That means they keep trying and don't give up—even when things get tough. And they're willing to work hard. They're also creative. Do you have that spirit?

Don't Be Afraid to Try—and to Fail

Entrepreneurs are risk takers. Not every idea works out. But an entrepreneur will simply try again or try something new. The important thing is being willing to take a chance. But before you abandon an idea, look carefully at your business and ask thoughtful questions about how you might be able to improve your sales.

Did you set up a lemonade stand and not make a single sale? What would happen if you moved to a busier spot?

Are your cupcakes getting stale before you can sell them? Would reducing the price make them sell more quickly? Can you still make a profit at the lower price?

Is the competition outpacing your dog-walking business? Are other dog walkers doing something you are not? Do they go out earlier in the morning? Can you spark some interest by running a promotion?

Are your handmade bracelets not selling as quickly as you'd like? Hold a **focus group**. Ask your customers what they like—and don't like. Take their advice. Think about creating some new designs.

Is an online store taking too much of your profit? Are there other options out there? Shop around for another already-created online store. Or set up your own online shop.

WORDS FROM WARREN

Persevering and learning from mistakes leads to success in finances and in life.

WORDS FROM WARREN

Be willing to change your ideas. Chains of habit are too light to be felt until they are too heavy to be broken.

focus group
a small number of people brought together to discuss a product or topic, answer questions about it, and offer up opinions and feedback

Be a Person of Integrity

Having **integrity** means being honest and fair and always striving to do the right thing. It is important in business and in life.

How would you feel if you hired someone to walk your dog but that person never showed up? Would you be upset if you bought a book online that the seller said was in good condition but it was falling apart when you got it? You probably wouldn't want to do business with that dog walker or bookseller again.

In business as in life, you will meet all kinds of people. Treat them with kindness—just like you want to be treated. Your customers, suppliers, and the people you work with will be thankful for it. Try to understand other people's points of view. Sometimes it is easier to understand and solve a problem by looking at it in a different way.

Be honest about what you can deliver. Be reliable. And be kind. Your customers will feel better about you and your business—and so will you!

integrity
being honest and fair

WORDS FROM WARREN

You can't make a good deal with a bad person.

Don't Be Afraid to Speak Up and Ask for What You Want

You have to speak up for the things you want—equipment, help, advice, money, a place to set up a table, and for new customers to take a chance on you. Identify a person who could help you and then make the strongest case you can to that person about why he or she should help. You may not always get what you ask for. In fact, the best businesspeople are used to not getting what they want every time they ask. But speaking up is a skill every business owner needs.

Henry Miller was fascinated by bees and worried about their survival. So he asked his parents for a beehive for his birthday. Pretty soon, his hive was producing honey, and he was selling his own honey by the side of the road. Now Henry's Humdingers is a real gourmet honey business with products—from Henry's own beehives—sold in his online store and in hundreds of natural food stores.

In order to make the cool bow ties he liked best, **Moziah Bridges** asked his grandmother for some fabric and for help in learning how to sew.

Emil Motycka asked his parents to cosign a loan so he could buy a commercial lawn mower and grow his business.

WORDS FROM WARREN

Try to find the job you'd have if you were independently rich. Forget about the pay. When you're associating with the people that you love, doing what you love, it doesn't get any better than that.

Cory Nieves, of Mr. Cory's Cookies, started his business by selling hot chocolate at a local pizza place. Then he made cookies and lemonade in his house and sold them from a stand outside. But the state health department has rules about how and where food can be cooked and sold. They shut down his business. Even when they got the bad news, Cory and his mom did not give up. They found a bakery that allowed them to use its commercial kitchen.

When **Anshul Samar** set out to create Elementeo, a fantasy board game that teaches players about chemistry, he reached out to The Indus Entrepreneurs (tie.org), a nonprofit that promotes entrepreneurship around the world, for advice. Members of the organization gave him advice on his business plan, marketing, and distribution. He was not afraid to ask for help and mentorship, and he ended up finding a lawyer and a public relations firm who did some work for his new product for free.

distribution
supplying goods to stores and businesses

Listen to Your Customers

Some of the best ideas in business can come straight from your customers. If you make and deliver pet food and one of your customers mentions that she's read that a grain-free diet is best for her dog breed, then add some grain-free recipes to your menu. When the mother of a child you tutor mentions an upcoming vacation, offer to put together a worksheet of fun exercises that the child can do in the car or on the trip. That way, you won't lose a week's worth of tutoring fees. By paying attention to your customers and thinking creatively, you will know to have bow ties or hair accessories made in their school colors right before a big game or pep rally.

After making the Elementeo board game, **Anshul Samar** added some do-it-yourself cards. He also created an app so that his customers could add chemistry-inspired characters to the game too.

Jake and **Lachlan Johnson**, of the two-part bow-tie business Beaux Up, ask their customers to send in their favorite pattern combinations.

WORDS FROM WARREN

I learned to go into business only with people whom I like, trust, and admire.

WORDS FROM WARREN

If you fail, try again. Failure is not falling down; it is staying down.

Stay Strong on the Bad Days

Mistakes and misunderstandings can happen in any business. If a customer isn't happy, offer them a refund and apologize. The thing that he or she will remember is not that you did a lousy job cleaning his car or bathing her dog, but that you were fair and nice to deal with. And if people like doing business with you, they will give you another chance.

Many young entrepreneurs have suffered through crowdfunding campaigns that didn't work. Or they've pitched their products to stores only to have them rejected. But that's just part of being an entrepreneur.

Be the Face of Your Business

Take pride in your hard work. When you enjoy what you do, it will show. Your customers will notice your enthusiasm. And don't forget that you can be your own best advertisement. If your product is wearable, wear it! If you offer a service, keep flyers, brochures, coupons, or a business card on you at all times.

Many of the young entrepreneurs in this book successfully represent their brands.

Use your product.
Leanna Archer loved taking care of her own hair and skin and started using recipes from her great-grandmother to make her all-natural products. Pretty soon, people were asking her what she used to make her hair look so wonderful.

Wear your wares.
Moziah Bridges wears his signature Mo's Bows bow ties everywhere he goes, and he looks great doing it.

Shout it out loud.
Lizzie Marie Likness tells people about her healthy cooking business whenever she can. "I'll tell the mailman, the cashier at our grocery store," she says, "or even the pizza delivery guy—but we rarely order pizza so that doesn't happen very often."

WORDS FROM WARREN
What I learned at an early age was to have the right habits early.

WORDS FROM WARREN
No matter how great the talent or efforts, some things just take time.

124

Be Patient

Get-rich-quick schemes are just what they sound like: too good to be true. Successful businesspeople must get in the habit of being patient. It can take a long time to grow a successful business.

After **Matthew Meyer** won the grand prize in the Warren Buffett's Secret Millionaires Club "Grow Your Own Business Challenge" in 2013 and the Fourth Grade First Prize and Chairman's Choice awards at the 2013 Cincinnati Invention Convention, he got a lot of press. But his product still needed some work. Originally called the Right-Writer, the product is like a glove that helps struggling writers hold a pen or pencil. Matthew found a flaw in the original design. So he and his mother worked with occupational therapists, educators, and designers to get the design just right. They learned a lot about pattern design and the process of manufacturing sewn goods. They worked with artists to create a logo and animated brand mascots. And they went through about 50 **prototypes**. Two years later, they are working toward securing funding to manufacture the product under the new name: Grip Wizard.

prototype
an original model of something that will be copied over and over again. The final product will be based on the **prototype**.

Matthew Meyer is taking the time to get his product right. And he is not the only young entrepreneur to think long-term. It took Anshul Samar three years to develop Elementeo. Gabrielle Jordan started making jewelry when she was 7 years old. She started her company at age 9 and launched the Jewelz of Jordan website at 11. Now, at 15, she continues to design and sell jewelry, she has written a book, and she's an in-demand speaker. She took it step-by-step and has built a strong business.

WORDS FROM WARREN

People would rather be promised a winning lottery ticket next week than an opportunity to get rich slowly.

Above All, Love What You Do and Have Fun

Tavi Gevinson loves fashion. Anshul Samar loves chemistry. Lizzie Marie Likness loves to bake. Moziah Bridges loves to look sharp and wanted to help other kids look great too. Juliette Brindak loved creating cool characters and sharing positive messages for girls. And Alina Morse of Zollipops loves healthy smiles. Their passion for their products and services helped to make their businesses successful.

People who start great businesses love their service or product, and they truly enjoy creating things. The wonderful thing about starting your own business is that you can make it whatever you want it to be. As an added bonus, you'll be more successful if you love your work and your business.

WORDS FROM WARREN

You really want to be in a place where you jump out of bed in the morning and you are all fired up to get to work.

WORDS FROM WARREN

Never give up searching for the job that you're passionate about.

RESOURCES

Websites and Blogs

The BizKid$ website includes profiles of young entrepreneurs and a kid-friendly blog about business: **bizkids.com/blog**

The U.S. Small Business Administration has some resources for young entrepreneurs: **sba.gov/content/young-entrepreneurs-series**

TheMint.org is dedicated to helping children manage their money wisely and learn good financial habits: **themint.org/kids**

In the money section of the PBS Kids website, you will find information about saving, managing, and earning money: **pbskids.org/itsmylife/money**

TIME For Kids magazine makes monthly editions of a magazine called *Your $: Financial Literacy for Kids*: **timeforkids.com/extras/financial%20literacy**

In the blog section of the Kidpreneurs website, you will find interviews with kids who have started businesses: **kidpreneurs.org/blog**

Videos and Podcasts

Listen to TED Talks by impressive kids and teens: **ted.com/playlists/129/ted_under_20**

Hear interviews with young entrepreneurs: **entrepreneurkidsacademy.com/category/podcasts**

Books

Better Than a Lemonade Stand! Small Business Ideas for Kids by Daryl Bernstein (Aladdin, 2012).

You Call the Shots: Succeed Your Way—and Live the Life You Want—with the 19 Essential Secrets of Entrepreneurship by Cameron Johnson with John David Mann (Free Press, 2007).

Start It Up: The Complete Teen Business Guide to Turning Your Passions into Pay by Kenrya Rankin (Zest Books, 2011).

Kidpreneurs: Young Entrepreneurs with Big Ideas! by Adam Toren and Matthew Toren (Business Plus Media, 2009).

The Making of a Young Entrepreneur: A Kid's Guide to Developing the Mind-Set for Success by Gabrielle J. Williams (Legacy Builder Group, 2011).

Games

bizkids.com/games

practicalmoneyskills.com/games

coolmath-games.com/1-business-games

financialentertainment.org

richkidsmartkid.com

Get Started with Square!

Using the Square Reader that comes with this book makes it easy to take credit card payments as well as cash. All you need is a Square Reader, a smartphone or tablet, and a product or service to sell.

→ Download the free Square app and sign in to your Square account.

→ Customize your Square app and add the products you sell.

→ Plug in your Square Reader and start taking payments.